Better Homes & Gardens®

# Annual Recipes 2017

Meredith® Consumer Marketing
Des Moines, Iowa

**DIRTY RICE-STUFFED TOMATOES**
*Recipe on page 205*

# *from the editor*

At *Better Homes & Gardens®* we're on a flavor quest to bring you some of the best food the world has to offer—from a 30-minute weeknight meal to a dinner party for friends.

For the first half of my life, I just might have been the pickiest eater in the world. I wouldn't eat tomatoes because the seeds are encased in a little packet of slime. I wouldn't eat fish (even fish sticks) because they might taste fishy. I wouldn't eat dark meat chicken because it had too much flavor. Yes, I said too much flavor. Add to these a long list of banned items that included beets, oatmeal, guacamole, sushi, onions, mushrooms, broccoli, lima beans, cooked fruit, and orange juice with any discernible pulp, and you have a picture of a West Texas boy who managed to survive on macaroni and cheese.

I've come a long way. Now I can hardly name a food I don't appreciate. OK, I'm not big on offal (organ meats) and I still pick whole anchovies off my Caesar salad. But most everything else I already love or I'm willing to try.

That's largely what *Better Homes & Gardens Annual Recipes 2017* is about. We are so enthusiastic about all the wonderful foods there are to experience that we want to spread the joy through the recipes and tantalizing photos in this book—a collection of all the recipes that appeared in *Better Homes & Gardens* magazine throughout the year. We believe there is always something new to try and, ultimately, to love. We hope as you page through this book, you'll find something that draws you to the kitchen—whether it's a recipe or photo that looks intriguing or a new take on an old favorite.

Stephen Orr, Editor in Chief
*Better Homes & Gardens* magazine

# Better Homes & Gardens.

# Annual Recipes 2017

Our seal assures you that every recipe in *Better Homes & Gardens. Annual Recipes 2017* has been tested in the Better Homes & Gardens. Test Kitchen. This means that each recipe is practical and reliable, and it meets our high standards of taste appeal. We guarantee your satisfaction with this book for as long as you own it.

All of us at Meredith Consumer Marketing are dedicated to providing you with information and ideas to enhance your home. We welcome your comments and suggestions. Write to us at: Meredith Consumer Marketing, 1716 Locust St., Des Moines, IA 50309-3023.

**Pictured on front cover:**
Carrot-Pecan Ice Cream Cake, recipe on page 226.

MEREDITH CONSUMER MARKETING
**Consumer Marketing Product Director:** Heather Sorensen
**Consumer Marketing Product Manager:** Tami Perkins
**Consumer Products Marketing Manager:** Wendy Merical
**Business Manager:** Diane Umland
**Senior Production Manager:** Al Rodruck

WATERBURY PUBLICATIONS, INC.
**Editorial Director:** Lisa Kingsley
**Associate Editor:** Tricia Bergman
**Creative Director:** Ken Carlson
**Associate Design Director:** Doug Samuelson
**Production Assistant:** Mindy Samuelson
**Contributing Copy Editors:** Terri Fredrickson, Peg Smith
**Contributing Indexer:** Mary Williams

*BETTER HOMES & GARDENS.* MAGAZINE
**Vice President, Editor in Chief:** Stephen Orr
**Editors:** Nancy Wall Hopkins, Jan Miller

MEREDITH CORPORATION
**Chairman and Chief Executive Officer:** Stephen M. Lacy

In Memoriam: E.T. Meredith III (1933–2003)

**MUSHROOM AND CHEESE
SOURDOUGH TOASTS**
*Recipe on page 45*

**ENCHILADA
CASSEROLE**
*Recipe on page 238*

**AUTHENTIC** Food, like fashion, has trends—some familiar and welcome, some worth adopting, others easily rejected. So it's comforting—and fun—to pick up a cookbook with approachable recipes, easy-to-find ingredients, and reliable instructions. That's what we've assembled for you in *Better Homes & Gardens Annual Recipes 2017.* And who better to learn from than BH&G food specialists, well-known chefs, cookbook authors, and food bloggers. Together they offer expertise, tips, and anecdotes to inspire cooking—from weekday meals to special occasions to experimenting with new foods and techniques. Many of these recipes call for fresh seasonal produce and uncomplicated preparation; some take a common food and serve it up in an entirely new and creative way. We're convinced you'll turn to these recipes again and again.

### LOOK FOR

**MONTHLY FEATURES** Never before have so many choices of cooking vessels—and recipes for them—been available. For cooking, smart pots, relative newcomers to the table, offer the combined convenience of speedy meals or all-day simmering. As sturdy standbys, well-seasoned cast-iron skillets dependably turn out favorite dishes from cornbread to skillet dinners. When produce is at its seasonal peak—spring asparagus, summer peaches or zucchini, for examples—food experts make the best of flavor, color, and texture. Culinary expert Genevieve Ko shares what's new in the world of spices; award-winning author and baker Dorie Greenspan reveals how to highlight irresistible fall flavors; and Joy the Baker swaps sweet for heat in recipes that have distinctive New Orleans-style.

**HOW TO COOK** Simplicity often yields the best results, and making pasta by hand stands to prove that less is more. Practice the techniques to turn out tender flavorful strands of deliciousness. For backyard grilling, taste how flavoring chicken wings with rubs and sauces guarantees rave reviews. Resolved to master the art of curing tough brisket for ultra-tender corned beef? The uncomplicated method simply involves a five-day brine. Then, follow the guidance of cookbook author Samin Nosrat for savory seasonal salsas.

**NEW WAYS** Expect the unexpected. This collection of recipes takes typical foods, such as cabbage, okra, and walnuts, and lets them shine in intriguing new ways. Red cabbage combined with buttery Yukon gold potatoes and Gruyère cheese results in a rich gratin. Okra tacos, you say? Fresh okra seasoned with chili powder, cumin, and coriander then quickly grilled over high heat, results in a tasty filling. Hearty protein-packed patties are a mix of meaty walnuts and lentils. Crisp jewel-tone radishes add color and mellow flavor to quiche, and carrots stand in for fettuccine in a pappardelle and creamy goat cheese dish.

**FAST & FRESH** While food is at its bountiful best, getting healthful weeknights meals in short time can be challenging. Rise to the occasion and confidently combine local market options of lean proteins, hearty grains, and fresh fruits and vegetables with these quick-to-the-table recipes. You'll serve delicious dinners from recipes that have been tested for freshness, taste, ease in preparation, healthful quality, and inspirational variety—and they're likely to become family favorites. These recipes and cooking techniques will show you the way.

MEXICAN CHILES
AND PEACHES
*Recipe on page 153*

# contents

42

95

270

**ZUCCHINI-WALNUT
CAKE**
*Recipe on page 188*

**HERB SALSA**
*Recipe on page 71*

SHORT RIB
GOULASH
*Recipe on page 28*

# january

Begin the year with cooking lessons: Delicate fresh pasta, fish steamed en papillote, and creative dishes with red cabbage that go beyond coleslaw. Then take it fast or slow with smart pots.

15    19    21

*how to cook*
# PASTA

Flour and eggs. That's all you need to make delicate strands of handmade pasta. Plus, the process of kneading and rolling is good for the soul.

**For generations,** northern Italian families have sat down to Sunday dinners of homemade egg pasta. Although kneading and rolling may sound like a big undertaking, fresh pasta hardly requires a recipe (and no special equipment). Just a little time and effort. Mix flour with eggs, knead until smooth, roll into thin sheets, and cut into whatever shape you like. The best news: Dough is extremely forgiving; you can't overwork it. The more you develop the gluten by kneading and rolling, the lighter, more tender the pasta.

In addition to fettuccine-like ribbons, this dough can be used for stuffed pastas such as ravioli and tortellini.

# PASTA BY HAND

*The combination of all-purpose flour and semolina makes a dough that is easy to work. Semolina's high protein provides good strength and elasticity to the dough.*

**MAKE THE WELL** On a clean work surface mix together 1 cup all-purpose flour and ¼ cup semolina flour. Form into a mound with a well in the center. Crack 2 eggs into the well (1).

**MIX THE DOUGH** Using a fork, gently beat the eggs, mixing in a tiny bit of flour with each stroke. Protect the well by using your opposite hand to build up the flour around the edge as you beat (2). Stir until the dough forms a lumpy mass. The mixture will be thick enough that you can no longer stir with a fork, but there will still be a few tablespoons flour on the surface.

**KNEAD UNTIL SMOOTH** At this point the dough will be very wet and sticky, so it's easy to start incorporating more flour with your fingertips (3). As the dough becomes drier and easier to work with, use your hands to knead (4) until smooth, firm, and elastic (5). (This will take about 10 minutes. Don't rush.) Cover with a clean towel. Let rest 20 minutes.

**ROLL THINLY** On a lightly floured surface roll dough into an 18-inch circle about ⅟₁₆ inch thick (6). (This will take some time and muscle!) Roll from the center out to ensure even thickness. You'll know the dough is thin enough when you see a faint outline of your hand through a lifted sheet of dough.

**CUT INTO STRIPS** Lightly flour the surface of the dough. Starting from the side closest to you, loosely roll into a spiral (7). Cut into ¼- to ½-inch-wide strips (8). They don't have to be perfect; that's part of the charm. Unfurl strips; sprinkle lightly with flour. Let stand 1 hour.

**COOK THE PASTA** In a large pot of boiling, salted water cook 2 to 3 minutes or until tender. There is no salt in the dough, be sure the water is well-salted. Drain well and serve with your choice of sauce.

**PASTA POSSIBILITIES** Add these colorful flavor enhancers to the flour along with the eggs. If the addition makes the dough too wet, toss in a tablespoon or two more all-purpose flour.

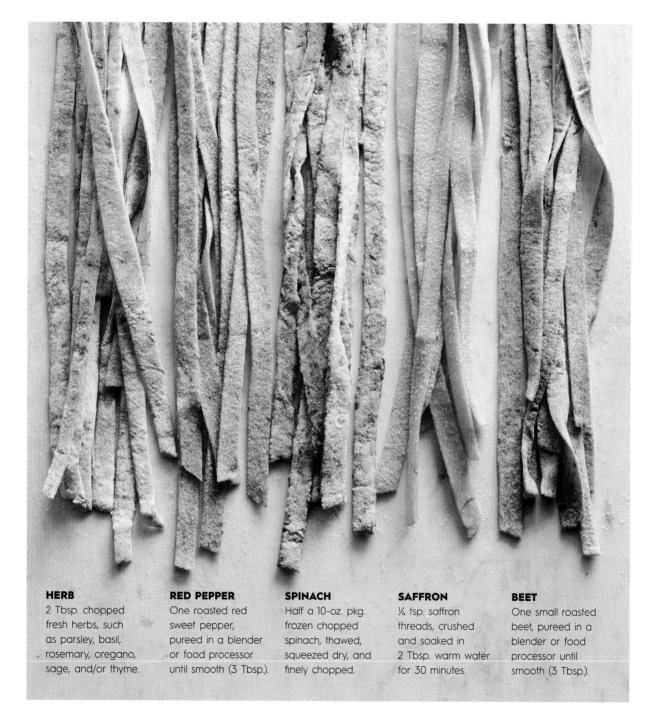

**HERB**
2 Tbsp. chopped fresh herbs, such as parsley, basil, rosemary, oregano, sage, and/or thyme.

**RED PEPPER**
One roasted red sweet pepper, pureed in a blender or food processor until smooth (3 Tbsp.).

**SPINACH**
Half a 10-oz. pkg. frozen chopped spinach, thawed, squeezed dry, and finely chopped.

**SAFFRON**
¼ tsp. saffron threads, crushed and soaked in 2 Tbsp. warm water for 30 minutes.

**BEET**
One small roasted beet, pureed in a blender or food processor until smooth (3 Tbsp.).

**THE RIGHT SAUCE** Less is more when it comes to saucing fresh pasta. You want to taste the pasta, after all. A few ideas: melted butter with slivered garlic and Parmigiano-Reggiano, chile oil with chopped fresh basil and parsley, or olive oil with lemon zest and capers.

# *new ways with* RED CABBAGE

Even if you never tire of coleslaw or stuffed cabbage rolls, these creative dishes will have you craving this humble, cruciferous vegetable.

Thanks to anthocyanin (a phytochemical found in purple foods), red cabbage provides the most nutrition of any cabbage. Look for round, compact heads that are heavy for their size. Waxy outer leaves should be crisp and tightly packed. Refrigerate in a plastic bag up to two weeks.

Red cabbage turns blue in reaction to some metals. To avoid this, cook in a nonreactive pan (no aluminum or cast iron) and don't use a carbon-steel knife. Pairing cabbage with acidic ingredients (lemon, vinegar, or wine) will preserve its gorgeous hue during the cooking.

CABBAGE AND BEEF
ROLLS

GRILLED CABBAGE
STEAKS WITH
CHIMICHURRI

CABBAGE AND
POTATO GRATIN

THE THICK, STURDY LEAVES OF RED CABBAGE REQUIRE LONGER COOKING TIME THAN GREEN OR WHITE. COOK JUST UNTIL TENDER; CABBAGE RELEASES STINKY HYDROGEN SULFIDE WHEN COOKED TOO LONG. ALSO AVOID BOILING, WHICH QUICKLY LEACHES OUT NUTRIENTS.

## CABBAGE AND POTATO GRATIN

**HANDS-ON TIME** 20 min.
**TOTAL TIME** 1 hour 20 min.

2     Tbsp. butter, softened
1½   lb. Yukon gold potatoes, thinly sliced
1     medium head cabbage, cored and shredded
½    cup shredded Gruyère
1½   cups whipping cream
2     Tbsp. chopped fresh thyme
3     cloves garlic, minced
½    cup panko bread crumbs
1     Tbsp. olive oil

**1.** Preheat oven to 425°F. Butter a 3-quart baking dish. In two layers add Yukon gold potatoes, cabbage, and Gruyère. In a bowl combine whipping cream, chopped thyme, garlic, and 1½ tsp. salt; pour over cabbage.
**2.** Cover; bake 30 minutes. Uncover; bake 15 minutes more. Sprinkle with panko mixed with olive oil. Bake 15 minutes more until golden brown. Makes 8 servings.
**PER SERVING** *312 cal, 23 g fat, 66 mg chol, 485 mg sodium, 21 g carb, 3 g fiber, 6 g pro.*

## GRILLED CABBAGE STEAKS WITH CHIMICHURRI

**HANDS-ON TIME** 35 min.
**TOTAL TIME** 45 min. plus overnight brine

6     cups water
⅓    cup kosher salt
⅓    cup sugar
3     sprigs rosemary
4     cups ice cubes
1     medium head red cabbage (about 2 lb.)
½    cup extra-virgin olive oil
2     Tbsp. snipped fresh rosemary
1     cup packed parsley leaves
¼    cup white wine vinegar
¼    cup coarsely chopped shallot
2     Tbsp. drained capers

**1.** In a large pot simmer the water, salt, sugar, and rosemary sprigs until salt and sugar dissolve; remove from heat. Add ice cubes. Add 1 cabbage cut into 4 steaks (reserve the two ends for another use). Chill overnight.
**2.** Drain cabbage; pat dry. Brush with ¼ cup olive oil; season with rosemary. Grill over medium heat 10 minutes, turning once.
**3.** Meanwhile, in a food processor combine parsley, vinegar, shallot, remaining olive oil, and drained capers until smooth. Serve with cabbage. Makes 4 servings.
**PER SERVING** *207 cal, 14 g fat, 0 mg chol, 567 mg sodium, 20 g carb, 5 g fiber, 4 g pro.*

## CABBAGE AND BEEF ROLLS

**HANDS-ON TIME** 25 min.
**TOTAL TIME** 40 min.

1     lb. trimmed, boneless beef sirloin
¼    medium head red cabbage, shredded (1½ cups)
1     bunch green onions, trimmed
1     Tbsp. toasted sesame seeds
1     Tbsp. vegetable oil
½    cup ponzu sauce*
      Toasted sesame seeds
      Shredded cabbage or butter lettuce

**1.** Pound beef sirloin into a 12×8-inch rectangle (¼ inch thick). Season with ½ tsp. freshly ground black pepper. Layer cabbage, green onions, and toasted sesame seeds across long side of beef. Roll up tightly; secure with toothpicks. Slice 1 inch thick.
**2.** In a large skillet heat vegetable oil over medium-high heat. Working in batches, cook slices 3 minutes per side then remove from skillet. Add ponzu sauce; cook 3 minutes, scraping up browned bits. Pour over slices. Sprinkle with toasted sesame seeds. Serve with shredded cabbage. Makes 4 servings.
***Tip** Or combine ¼ cup soy sauce and ¼ cup orange juice.
**PER SERVING** *245 cal, 9 g fat, 78 mg chol, 791 mg sodium, 13 g carb, 4 g fiber, 29 g pro.*

# FAST & FRESH

Easy, healthful recipes for a better dinner tonight.

## PARCHMENT-BAKED FISH WITH LEMONGRASS

*Lemongrass has a fibrous, woody texture. Use the back of a knife to crush the stalk before mincing. As an alternative, use an equal amount of purchased lemongrass paste.*

**HANDS-ON TIME** 30 min.
**TOTAL TIME** 45 min.

6    green onions
2    stalks fresh lemongrass, trimmed, smashed, and minced (¼ cup)
1    Tbsp. minced fresh ginger
2    tsp. canola oil
2    cups thinly sliced button mushrooms
2    red and/or orange sweet peppers, cut into strips
     Sriracha sauce
4    4- to 6-oz. ½-inch-thick skinless white fish fillets, such as hake or cod*
1    lime, halved
     Fresh cilantro sprigs

**1.** Preheat oven to 400°F. Finely chop 4 green onions. In a small bowl combine chopped green onions, lemongrass, ginger, and oil; set aside. Cut four 15-inch lengths of parchment paper. Fold each in half like a book, creasing the center. Open papers and spread an even amount of lemongrass mixture across the center of one side of each paper.

**2.** Cut the remaining green onions into 2-inch pieces. Evenly top lemongrass mixture with green onions, mushrooms, and peppers. Drizzle lightly with sriracha. Place fish on vegetables; add a squeeze of lime juice. Season with salt. Top with cilantro.

**3.** Fold parchment over food. To seal packets, start at bottom folded edge and crease the corner up at an angle. Working in 2-inch sections, continue creasing open edges, overlapping each fold. Crease folds tightly to stay closed. Finish by tucking the last flap underneath packet (packet will be a half-moon shape). Transfer filled packets to a baking sheet. Bake 15 to 20 minutes.* Make a narrow slit and check whether fish flakes easily when tested with a fork. (Bake 1 to 2 minutes more, if needed.) Open packets carefully to serve. Makes 4 servings.

**\*Tip** If fish fillets are ¾ to 1 inch thick, increase baking time to 20 to 25 minutes.

**EACH SERVING** *163 cal, 3 g fat, 49 mg chol, 279 mg sodium, 11 g carb, 2 g fiber, 23 g pro.*

PARCHMENT PACKETS SEAL IN BOLD, SPICY FLAVORS OF GINGER, SRIRACHA, AND LEMONGRASS TO YIELD AROMATIC BROTH AND PERFECTLY TENDER FISH.

WINTER BULGUR SALAD
WITH OLIVE DRESSING

## HONEY-GLAZED PORK AND FENNEL

*When working with fennel, first remove stalks, then cut the bulb in half lengthwise through the core, then slice into wedges. If you have extra fronds after mixing the glaze, use them as a pretty garnish.*

**HANDS-ON TIME** 15 min.
**TOTAL TIME** 50 min.

- 1½ to 1¾ lb. pork tenderloin
- ⅓ cup cider vinegar
- ⅓ cup honey
- 1 Tbsp. Dijon-style mustard
- 4 cloves garlic, coarsely chopped
- 2 Tbsp. extra-virgin olive oil
- 2 medium fennel bulbs, trimmed and cut into ¾-inch wedges, fronds reserved
  Microgreens or fresh herbs (optional)

**1.** Preheat oven to 425°F. Line a 15×10×1-inch baking pan or small roasting pan with foil. Place pork in pan; season with salt and black pepper on all sides.
**2.** For glaze, in a small bowl whisk together vinegar, honey, mustard, and garlic. While whisking, slowly stream in olive oil. Chop reserved fennel fronds (up to ½ cup); stir into glaze.
**3.** Pour glaze over pork. Add fennel wedges to pan; toss in glaze to coat. Roast 30 to 35 minutes or until pork is done (145°F). Cover with foil. Let rest 5 minutes before slicing. Top with microgreens or fresh herbs. Makes 4 servings.
**EACH SERVING** *356 cal, 8 g fat, 111 mg chol, 310 mg sodium, 33 g carb, 4 g fiber, 37 g pro.*

## WINTER BULGUR SALAD WITH OLIVE DRESSING

*For a light take on all-grain salads, this base uses equal parts bulgur and chopped cauliflower.*

**TOTAL TIME** 25 min.

- 1 cup bulgur
- 2 cups boiling water
- ½ medium head cauliflower, chopped, (2 cups)
- ½ cup pitted Kalamata and/or green olives, coarsely chopped
- 3 Tbsp. fresh lemon juice
- 3 Tbsp. extra-virgin olive oil
- 1 clove garlic, minced
- 4 cups torn chicories (escarole, radicchio, and/or endive)
- 6 celery stalks, thinly bias sliced
- 4 oz. feta cheese, crumbled

**1.** Place bulgur in a large heatproof bowl. Pour the boiling water over bulgur; cover. Let stand 15 minutes.
**2.** Meanwhile, place cauliflower in a food processor. Pulse three to five times, just until finely chopped.
**3.** For Olive Dressing, in a small bowl stir together olives, lemon juice, olive oil, and garlic. Season with black pepper to taste.
**4.** Drain bulgur; return to bowl. Stir in cauliflower. Arrange the bulgur mixture, chicories, celery, and cheese on a platter. Serve with Olive Dressing. Makes 4 servings.
**EACH SERVING** *361 cal, 21 g fat, 25 mg chol, 744 mg sodium, 35 g carb, 8 g fiber, 10 g pro.*

HONEY-GLAZED
PORK AND FENNEL

CHEESY ITALIAN
BAKED BEANS

# CRIMSON CUTOUTS

Craft the heart stencils for these Valentine's Day cookies out of cardstock.

## RED VELVET HEART COOKIES

**HANDS-ON TIME** 40 min.
**TOTAL TIME** 2 hr.

| | |
|---|---|
| 1 | cup butter, softened |
| 1¼ | cups granulated sugar |
| 2 | Tbsp. unsweetened cocoa powder |
| 1½ | tsp. baking powder |
| 2 | eggs |
| 1 | Tbsp. liquid red food coloring |
| 1 | tsp. vanilla |
| 2¾ | cups all-purpose flour |
| | Powdered sugar |

**1.** In a large mixing bowl beat butter on medium to high 30 seconds. Add sugar, cocoa, baking powder, and ½ tsp. salt.
**2.** Beat until combined, scraping sides of bowl occasionally. Beat in eggs, food coloring, and vanilla until combined. Beat in as much of the flour as you can with the mixer. Stir in any remaining flour. Divide dough in half. Cover; chill dough 1 hour or until easy to handle.
**3.** Preheat oven to 375°F. On a floured surface roll half the dough at a time to ¼-inch thickness. Cut dough using a 2½- to 3½-inch heart-shape cookie cutter. Place cutouts 1 inch apart on ungreased cookie sheets.
**4.** Bake 6 to 7 minutes or until edges are firm and bottoms are very light brown. Transfer cookies to wire racks to cool. Sprinkle with powdered sugar, using stencils if desired. Makes forty-six 2½-inch or twenty-two 3½-inch cookies.
**EACH SERVING** *86 cal, 4 g fat, 19 mg chol, 76 mg sodium, 11 g carb, 0 g fiber, 1 g pro.*

# GAME-DAY CHILI

Fill the toppings bar with bowls of chopped red onions, sour cream, oyster crackers, and shredded cheddar cheese.

## BOWL O'RED

*This Bowl o'Red stands out for what it doesn't contain: beans. Ground beef, tomatoes, and a generous amount of medium-hot pasilla chile pepper make this a one-pot winner.*

**HANDS-ON TIME** 20 min.
**TOTAL TIME** 40 min.

| | |
|---|---|
| 1¼ | lb. ground beef chuck |
| 1 | cup chopped onion |
| 3 | cloves garlic, minced |
| 1 | Tbsp. ground pasilla or ancho chile pepper |
| 1 | tsp. ground cumin |
| 1 | tsp. paprika |
| 1 | tsp. dried oregano, crushed |
| ¼ | tsp. cayenne pepper |
| ⅛ | tsp. ground cloves |
| 1 | 14.5-oz. can diced tomatoes, undrained |
| 1 | 14.5-oz. can beef broth |
| 1 | 12-oz. bottle lager beer or 1½ cups beef broth |
| 1 | Tbsp. yellow mustard |

**1.** In a Dutch oven cook ground beef, onion, and garlic over medium-high heat until meat is browned, breaking up meat. Drain off fat. Stir in pasilla pepper, cumin, paprika, oregano, cayenne pepper, cloves, and 1 tsp. salt. Cook and stir 2 to 3 minutes or until fragrant.

**2.** Stir in tomatoes, broth, beer, and mustard. Bring to boiling; reduce heat. Simmer, uncovered, about 40 minutes. Makes 6 servings.

**EACH SERVING** *379 cal, 25 g fat, 97 mg chol, 916 mg sodium, 10 g carb, 2 g fiber, 24 g pro.*

**Slow Cooker** Prepare as directed in Step 1. Transfer to a 4-quart slow cooker. Stir in tomatoes, broth, ½ cup of the beer, and the mustard. Cover. Cook on low 8 to 10 hours or on high 4 to 5 hours.

SUMMER
CHERRY TOMATO
AND OLIVE TART
*Recipe on page 63*

# march

Celebrate springlike days with a nod to light flavors, buttery tarts with sweet or savory fillings, and a lesson on corned beef—just in time for a St. Patrick's Day celebration.

54    57    59

*how to cook*
# CORNED BEEF

With the craze among food-lovers for all things cured, this briny classic is poised for a comeback.

**CORNED BEEF** is a tough cut of meat (often brisket) cured in a brine then boiled over low heat for several hours. The result: salty, tender deliciousness. No corn (of the cob variety) is involved; rather, the term corned comes from the Old English for grain, referring in this case to the typically large grains of salt used to preserve the meat. Curing beef at home is surprisingly straightforward, but it isn't fast. The secret to ultratender meat lies in a five-day brine.

**1** **PICKLING SPICE** Delicious corned beef starts with a good quality pickling spice. Our blend is a robust riff on a classic combination of spices; play around as you would with a BBQ rub, tweaking amounts or adding heat to suit your taste.

**2** **BRINE** Pink curing salt (sodium nitrite) is the one uncommon ingredient worth seeking out for the way it tenderizes the meat and gives it that bright pink color. Look for brands like DQ Curing Salt and Prague Mix No. 1 at your local butcher or online.

**3** **BRISKET** This is an inexpensive cut from the pectoral muscles, often sold as flat or point cuts. For corned beef, we opt for the flat, which is less fatty than the point, which is easier to slice.

# CORNED BEEF

**HANDS-ON TIME** 45 min.
**TOTAL TIME** 3 hr. 45 min., plus brine time

### PICKLING SPICE
- 2   Tbsp. mustard seeds
- 2   Tbsp. coriander seeds
- 1   Tbsp. black peppercorns
- 1   Tbsp. whole allspice
- 1   Tbsp. whole cloves
- 8   whole cardamom pods
- 2   cinnamon sticks, broken into pieces
- 4   bay leaves, crumbled
- 1   tsp. ground ginger
- 1   tsp. crushed red pepper (optional)

### BRINE
- 1   gallon water
- 2   cups kosher salt
- 1   Tbsp. pink curing salt
- 4   cloves garlic, minced
- ½   cup packed brown sugar
- 1   recipe Pickling Spice, *above*

### CORNED BEEF
- 1   3½- to 4-lb. flat cut beef brisket
- 1   medium head cabbage, cut into wedges
- 1   onion, coarsely chopped
- 4   carrots, cut into 2-inch pieces

**1.** For Pickling Spice, in a small bowl combine all ingredients. Set aside.
**2.** For Brine, in a large pot combine the water, kosher and pink salts, garlic, brown sugar, and ¼ cup Pickling Spice. Bring to a simmer, stirring until sugar is dissolved. Remove from heat. Let stand until room temperature. Transfer to a 2-gallon resealable plastic bag set in a large shallow pan.
**3.** For Corned Beef, place brisket in bag; seal. Chill 5 days, turning occasionally.
**4.** Remove brisket from brine; rinse thoroughly. Transfer to an 8- to 10-quart pot. Cover with fresh water. Place remaining Pickling Spice on a double-thick 8-inch square of 100% cotton cheesecloth. Bring up corners; tie with 100% cotton string. Add to pot with beef. Bring to boiling; reduce heat to low. Simmer, covered, 3 hours or until brisket is fork tender, adding cabbage, onion, and carrots the last 15 minutes. Remove spice bag; discard. Thinly slice corned beef.

Serve with cabbage, onion, and carrots. Makes 6 servings plus leftovers.
**EACH SERVING** *198 cal, 8 g fat, 55 mg chol, 1,064 mg sodium, 14 g carb, 5 g fiber, 19 g pro.*

## ULTIMATE MELT

*Let this gooey melt be your jumping-off place for using corned beef leftovers, knowing that hash, pizza, and pasta are yet to be had. The tantalizing flavor for this Reuben sandwich is the pickled onions, which soak in leftover cooking liquid from the corned beef.*

**HANDS-ON TIME** 20 min.
**TOTAL TIME** 1 hr. 30 min.

- 1   cup leftover Corned Beef cooking liquid
- ¼   cup apple cider vinegar
- 1   Tbsp. granulated sugar
- ¾   cup thinly sliced red onion
- 12  slices marble rye bread
- 6   to 12 Tbsp. butter
- 3   Tbsp. Dijon-style mustard
- 6   Tbsp. Thousand Island dressing
- 1½  cups shredded fontina cheese
- 1½  lb. corned beef

**1.** For the pickled onions, in a saucepan combine cooking liquid, vinegar, and sugar. Bring to boiling. Place the onion slices in a medium heatproof bowl; pour the vinegar mixture over top. Let stand 1 hour; drain and discard the liquid.
**2.** Spread butter on one side of each bread slice and mustard and Thousand Island dressing on the other side. Top three bread slices, buttered sides down, with corned beef, cheese, and pickled onions. Top with remaining bread slices, buttered sides up.
**3.** Preheat a large skillet over medium heat. Cook sandwiches 4 to 6 minutes or until toasted and cheese is melted, turning once. Makes 6 sandwiches.

*new ways with*
# WALNUTS

Even favorite combos deserve a little reinvention now and then.

High fat content gives walnuts both nutritional oomph (it's the good-for-you polyunsaturated fat) and a buttery taste that pairs well with astringent flavors (bitter vegetables and tart fruits). Mild tannins in the skins balance sweet and rich dishes (fatty meats and creamy pastas).

GINGER PORK
CHOPS WITH
CURRIED WALNUTS

WALNUT
LENTIL
PATTIES

CREAMY WALNUT
PASTA

BECAUSE OF THE HIGH FAT, WALNUTS SPOIL QUICKLY AT ROOM TEMPERATURE. THEY KEEP FOR ONE MONTH IN THE FRIDGE OR ONE YEAR IN THE FREEZER.

## GINGER PORK CHOPS WITH CURRIED WALNUTS

**TOTAL TIME** 40 min.

2   cups steamed butternut squash
2   Tbsp. vegetable oil
1   cup walnuts
½   tsp. curry powder
⅛   tsp. cayenne pepper
4   ½-inch thick boneless pork chops (5 oz. each)
1   small red onion, cut into thin wedges
1   orange, zested and juiced (¼ cup juice and 1 Tbsp. zest)
¼   cup reduced-sodium soy sauce
1   Tbsp. honey
1   Tbsp. grated fresh ginger
    Fresh thyme (optional)

**1.** Place a steamer basket in a large saucepan; add water to just below the basket. Bring water to boiling; add squash. Cover; steam over medium heat 10 minutes or until squash is tender. Set aside.
**2.** Meanwhile, in a large skillet heat 1 Tbsp. of the oil over medium heat. Add walnuts, curry powder, and cayenne. Cook and stir 5 minutes; transfer to a small bowl. Heat remaining 1 Tbsp. oil in the skillet over medium heat. Add pork chops and onion. Cook 7 minutes or until pork is done (145°F), turning once.
**3.** In a small bowl stir together orange zest and juice, soy sauce, honey, and ginger; add to skillet along with butternut squash. Bring to boiling; heat through. Top with the spiced walnuts and, if desired, fresh thyme. Makes 4 servings.
**EACH SERVING** *508 cal, 30 g fat, 79 mg chol, 678 mg sodium, 22 g carb, 5 g fiber, 41 g pro.*

## CREAMY WALNUT PASTA

**TOTAL TIME** 25 min.

1½   cups half-and-half
1¼   cups walnut pieces
6    cloves garlic, peeled
1    9-oz. pkg. refrigerated fettuccine
4    slices bacon
4    eggs
¼    cup chopped Italian parsley

**1.** For the sauce, in a blender combine half-and-half, ¾ cup of the walnuts, garlic, and ½ tsp. each salt and pepper. Blend until nearly smooth. Pour into a large saucepan. Warm over low heat.
**2.** Meanwhile, cook fettuccine according to package directions; drain. Keep warm.
**3.** In an extra- large skillet cook bacon over medium heat until crisp; drain on paper towels. Add remaining ¾ cup walnuts to bacon drippings in skillet. Cook and stir 1 minute; use a slotted spoon to transfer walnuts to paper towels. Reserve 1 Tbsp. drippings in skillet.
**4.** For the fried eggs, break eggs into skillet; reduce heat to low. Cover; cook eggs for 3 to 4 minutes or until whites are completely set and yolks start to thicken.
**5.** Toss cooked pasta with sauce. Sprinkle with the crumbled bacon, walnuts, and parsley. Serve with fried eggs. Season with additional salt and pepper. Makes 4 servings.
**EACH SERVING** *688 cal, 45 g fat, 265 mg chol, 679 mg sodium, 46 g carb, 5 g fiber, 25 g pro.*

## WALNUT LENTIL PATTIES

**HANDS-ON TIME** 25 min.
**TOTAL TIME** 1 hr.

     Water
½    cup dry lentils
4    Tbsp. olive oil
2    cups thinly sliced miniature sweet peppers
6    oz. mushrooms, finely chopped
1    cup walnut pieces
1    tsp. herbes de Provence
½    cup bread crumbs
1    egg, lightly beaten
8    slices country bread
¼    cup mayonnaise
     Fresh basil leaves

**1.** In a medium saucepan combine the water and lentils. Bring to boiling; reduce heat. Simmer, covered, 30 minutes or until very soft. Drain any excess water.
**2.** In an extra-large skillet heat 1 Tbsp. olive oil over medium-high heat; add sweet peppers. Cook 5 minutes or until tender. Remove from skillet; set aside. In the same skillet heat 1 Tbsp. oil over medium heat. Add mushrooms; cook and stir 6 to 8 minutes or until tender and liquid has evaporated. Transfer to a food processor. Add 1 cup cooked lentils, ½ cup walnuts, herbes de Provence, and ½ tsp. each salt and black pepper. Pulse until smooth.
**3.** In a large bowl combine bread crumbs and egg. Stir in lentil mixture. Stir in an additional 1 cup cooked lentils. Shape into four ½-inch-thick patties. Press remaining ½ cup walnuts into patties. In the same skillet heat remaining 2 Tbsp. oil over medium heat. Add patties; cook 3 minutes per side or until lightly browned and heated through. Serve patties on bread with mayonnaise, basil, and sautéed peppers. Makes 4 servings.
**EACH SERVING** *448 cal, 32 g fat, 47 mg chol, 425 mg sodium, 31 g carb, 6 g fiber, 15 g pro.*

# FAST & FRESH

Easy, healthful recipes for a better dinner tonight.

**GRILLED SALMON AND LEEKS WITH ROSEMARY-MUSTARD BUTTER**

## GRILLED SALMON AND LEEKS WITH ROSEMARY-MUSTARD BUTTER

*Washing leeks requires extra attention because the leaves hold on to grit. Wash thoroughly by shaking and separating the leaves while they are submerged in cold water.*

**TOTAL TIME** 30 min.

- 1½ lb. leeks
- 2 Tbsp. olive oil
- 1 sprig rosemary
- 4 4- to 6-oz. skin-on salmon fillets, ¾ to 1 inch thick
- ¼ cup unsalted butter, softened
- 2 tsp. Dijon-style mustard

**1.** Trim dark green tops and root ends from leeks, leaving ends intact. Cut leeks in half lengthwise; peel off tough outer leaves. Wash leeks; pat dry. (Keep some water on leeks to prevent burning on the grill.) Brush with 1 Tbsp. oil; season with ¼ tsp. each salt and black pepper.
**2.** On a grill or grill pan over medium-high heat, grill rosemary sprig 1 to 2 minutes or until lightly charred; remove. Grill the leeks 5 to 7 minutes or until tender, turning occasionally. Remove; cover to keep warm.
**3.** Season salmon with ¼ tsp. each salt and black pepper; brush with remaining olive oil. Grill fish, skin sides up, 4 minutes; turn. Grill 2 minutes or until fish flakes easily with a fork. Remove from heat.
**4.** Strip rosemary leaves from stem; chop leaves. In a small bowl stir together butter, mustard, and 1 tsp. chopped leaves. Spread butter on fish and leeks; sprinkle with remaining chopped rosemary. Makes 4 servings.
**EACH SERVING** *369 cal, 26 g fat, 93 mg chol, 415 mg sodium, 11 g carb, 1 g fiber, 24 g pro.*

**SWEET POTATOES AND BOK CHOY WITH MISO DRESSING**

## SWEET POTATOES AND BOK CHOY WITH MISO DRESSING

*Miso, the Japanese paste made from fermented soybeans and barley or rice malt, comes in red, white, or yellow varieties—red is the most pungent.*

**HANDS-ON TIME** 15 min.
**TOTAL TIME** 30 min.

- 1½ lb. assorted colored sweet potatoes, peeled and cut into 1-inch chunks
- 6 heads baby bok choy, halved lengthwise
- ¼ cup minced fresh ginger
- 2 Tbsp. red or brown miso paste
- 2 Tbsp. lime juice
- 2 Tbsp. cider vinegar
- 2 tsp. maple syrup
- 2 cloves garlic, minced
- 6 Tbsp. canola oil
  Cooked red or white quinoa
  Sesame seeds (optional)

**1.** Place a steamer basket in a large skillet or pot. Add water to just below the basket. Bring to boiling; reduce heat. Add sweet potatoes to basket; cover. Steam 10 minutes. Add bok choy; cover. Steam 5 minutes more or until tender.
**2.** Meanwhile, for Miso Dressing, in a small bowl whisk together the ginger, miso, lime juice, cider vinegar, maple syrup, and garlic. Gradually whisk in canola oil until combined.
**3.** Serve veggies over quinoa; drizzle with Miso Dressing. Sprinkle with sesame seeds, if desired. Makes 4 servings.
**EACH SERVING** *492 cal, 23 g fat, 515 mg sodium, 64 g carb, 10 g fiber, 10 g pro.*

**CREAMY RICOTTA SPAGHETTINI WITH ARUGULA**

## MOROCCAN CHICKEN AND PEPPERS

*No ingredient is more emblematic of Moroccan cuisine than harissa, a North African chile paste. It provides depth of heat to staples such as chicken and couscous.*

**HANDS-ON TIME** 30 min.
**TOTAL TIME** 45 min.

| | |
|---|---|
| 1 | tsp. coriander seeds |
| 1 | tsp. cumin seeds |
| 1 | to 2 small dried red chiles (such as chile de árbol), torn into pieces |
| ¼ | tsp. ground cinnamon |
| 8 | skinless, boneless chicken thighs |
| 2 | Tbsp. olive oil |
| 6 | cups coarsely chopped sweet peppers (red, orange, or yellow) |
| 1 | Meyer or regular lemon, sliced |
| | Harissa paste |

**1.** In a spice grinder or with a mortar and pestle, grind coriander, cumin, and chiles; stir in cinnamon and ½ tsp. salt. Sprinkle mixture over chicken.
**2.** In a 12-inch skillet heat olive oil over medium-high heat 1 to 2 minutes. Cook chicken 15 to 17 minutes or until done (170°F). Remove to a platter; cover to keep warm. Add peppers and lemon slices to skillet. Cook 6 to 8 minutes or until peppers and lemon slices are tender and lightly browned, stirring occasionally. Add to platter with chicken. Serve with harissa paste. Makes 4 servings.
**EACH SERVING** *443 cal, 19 g fat, 266 mg chol, 569 mg sodium, 7 g carb, 3 g fiber, 57 g pro.*

## CREAMY RICOTTA SPAGHETTINI WITH ARUGULA

*Peppery arugula wilts slightly when tossed with the warm pasta. Other tender greens—baby spinach or kale— would be equally delicious.*

**TOTAL TIME** 20 min.

| | |
|---|---|
| 8 | oz. dried spaghettini |
| 2 | Tbsp. olive oil |
| ¾ | cup roasted, salted, shelled pistachios, chopped |
| 1 | clove garlic, minced |
| 1 | cup ricotta cheese |
| ½ | cup grated Parmesan cheese |
| 5 | oz. arugula |

**1.** In a large pot cook pasta according to package directions. Drain, reserving 1 cup pasta water. Return pasta to pot.
**2.** Meanwhile, in a large skillet heat oil 2 minutes over medium-high heat. Add pistachios and garlic; cook 2 minutes or until lightly toasted. Stir ricotta, ¼ tsp. salt, and ½ cup pasta water into skillet until smooth and heated through. Transfer sauce to pot; stir in Parmesan. Add remaining pasta water; toss pasta until sauce is creamy. Gently toss in arugula. Top with black pepper and additional pistachios. Makes 4 servings.
**EACH SERVING** *562 cal, 30 g fat, 40 mg chol, 489 mg sodium, 53 g carb, 5 g fiber, 23 g pro.*

MOROCCAN CHICKEN
AND PEPPERS

SUMMER
CHERRY TOMATO
AND OLIVE TART

## CHICKEN SALTIMBOCCA

*This riff on saltimbocca—an Italian dish of veal, prosciutto, and sage—uses chicken, pancetta, and marjoram for an easy and approachable take on the original. Pounding chicken breasts until thin ensures quick and even cooking. Seal each chicken breast in a plastic bag and pound with a meat mallet to ½-inch thickness.*

**HANDS-ON TIME** 35 min.
**TOTAL TIME** 50 min.

2   Tbsp. olive oil
8   thin slices pancetta
4   skinless, boneless chicken breast halves (6 to 8 oz. each), pounded to ½-inch thickness
2   Tbsp. fresh marjoram or oregano leaves
1   fennel bulb, trimmed, halved, cored, and thinly sliced
1   small red onion, thinly sliced

**1.** Preheat oven to 375°F. In an extra-large skillet heat 1 Tbsp. olive oil over medium heat. Add pancetta slices; cook 30 to 60 seconds or until they start to brown. Remove from skillet. Increase heat to medium-high.
**2.** Season chicken with ¼ tsp. each salt and black pepper. Add chicken to skillet; cook 4 to 5 minutes until golden. Turn; cook 1 minute more. Transfer to a shallow baking pan. Top with 1 Tbsp. marjoram and the pancetta.
**3.** Bake 12 to 15 minutes or until chicken is done (165°F). Meanwhile, in a medium bowl toss together fennel and onion. Drizzle with remaining 1 Tbsp. olive oil; season with ¼ tsp. each salt and black pepper. Serve with chicken. Sprinkle with remaining marjoram. Makes 4 servings.
**EACH SERVING** *377 cal, 20 g fat, 136 mg chol, 575 mg sodium, 6 g carb, 2 g fiber, 42 g pro.*

CHEESY BAKED GNOCCHI WITH KALE

## CHEESY BAKED GNOCCHI WITH KALE

*Gnocchi and kale get French treatment when baked in a rich béchamel sauce. Find fresh, frozen, or shelf-stable packaged gnocchi in potato, whole wheat, and semolina varieties.*

**HANDS-ON TIME** 25 min.
**TOTAL TIME** 40 min.

2    16-oz. pkg. gnocchi
10   oz. kale, washed, stemmed, and chopped (6 cups)
3    cloves garlic, minced
2    Tbsp. butter
2    Tbsp. all-purpose flour
1½   cups milk
2    oz. Fontina or sharp white cheddar cheese, shredded (½ cup)
1    Tbsp. lemon zest
½    cup finely shredded Parmesan

**1.** Preheat oven to 400°F. Grease a 2-quart baking dish; set aside. In a 6-quart pot cook gnocchi according to package directions, adding kale the last 1 minute. Drain; return to pot.
**2.** Meanwhile, in a saucepan cook garlic in butter over medium heat for 1 minute. Stir in flour to combine. Whisk in milk; cook and stir until thickened and bubbly. Stir in Fontina and lemon zest. Pour over gnocchi and kale; stir to coat. Transfer to prepared baking dish. Top with Parmesan. Bake 20 minutes until lightly browned and bubbly. Makes 6 servings.
**EACH SERVING** *444 cal, 11 g fat, 31 mg chol, 749 mg sodium, 71 g carb, 4 g fiber, 18 g pro.*

SPRING
MINESTRONE

## BUTTERY POACHED SHRIMP SALAD

*This salad is far from a simple bed of mixed greens. The combo of shrimp, beets, and potatoes adds bulk to Bibb lettuce, and lemon-butter dressing perks up the salad with bright and rich flavors. The poaching liquid cooks the shrimp at a gentle heat to ensure good texture. Add parsley or celery leaves, citrus peel, or chopped carrots to infuse the liquid with extra flavor.*

**HANDS-ON TIME** 20 min.
**TOTAL TIME** 45 min.

8   oz. red and/or yellow beets, peeled and sliced ¼ inch thick
2   Tbsp. olive oil
1¼  lb. tiny yellow new potatoes, halved
1   lb. fresh or frozen large shrimp in shells, peeled and deveined
3   Tbsp. butter
1   lemon (1 tsp. zest and 3 Tbsp. juice)
2   Tbsp. chopped fresh chives
1   head Bibb lettuce, torn into small pieces

**1.** Preheat oven to 400°F. Line a baking sheet with foil. Arrange beet slices on baking sheet. Brush with 1 Tbsp. olive oil. Roast 20 to 25 minutes or until tender.
**2.** Meanwhile, in a large pot cook potatoes in lightly salted boiling water for 15 minutes or until tender. Using a slotted spoon, transfer potatoes to a large bowl.
**3.** Reduce heat to medium-low. Add shrimp to pot. Cook 2 to 3 minutes or until opaque. Transfer shrimp to a second large bowl; empty pot. In the same pot melt butter; stir in lemon zest and juice, chives, remaining 1 Tbsp. olive oil, and ½ tsp. freshly cracked black pepper. Return shrimp to pot; toss to coat. Arrange beets and potatoes on lettuce; top with shrimp. Sprinkle with additional chopped chives, if desired. Makes 4 servings.
**EACH SERVING** *351 cal, 16 g fat, 182 mg chol, 255 mg sodium, 30 g carb, 6 g fiber, 24 g pro.*

## SPRING MINESTRONE

*Tender baby greens are one of the first signs of spring. Let farmers market finds inspire this lighter, greener take on minestrone. Choose any combination of greens, including baby spinach, chard, dandelion, or arugula. They will keep in the refrigerator up to one week when wrapped in paper towels and sealed in a plastic bag.*

**HANDS-ON TIME** 20 min.
**TOTAL TIME** 40 min.

2   Tbsp. olive oil
1   medium leek, thinly sliced
2   cloves garlic, minced
3   cups reduced-sodium chicken broth
1   bay leaf
1   15- to 16-oz. can Great Northern or cannellini beans, rinsed and drained
1   bunch (8 oz.) asparagus, washed, trimmed, and cut into 2-inch pieces
3   cups coarsely chopped spring greens
4   slices sourdough or French bread
2   oz. aged goat cheese, crumbled, or Parmesan cheese, shredded (½ cup)

**1.** In a large pot heat 1 Tbsp. olive oil over medium heat. Add leek, garlic, and ¼ tsp. salt. Cook and stir 5 minutes or until tender. Stir in broth, 2 cups water, and bay leaf; bring to boiling. Stir in beans and asparagus. Return to boiling; reduce heat. Simmer, uncovered, 3 to 4 minutes or until asparagus is tender. Remove bay leaf. Stir in greens.
**2.** Meanwhile, for cheese toasts, preheat broiler. Brush remaining 1 Tbsp. olive oil on each side of bread. Arrange on a baking sheet. Broil 3 to 4 inches from heat for 1 minute on each side. Sprinkle with cheese; broil 1 minute or until lightly browned. Serve with soup. Makes 4 servings.
**EACH SERVING** *292 cal, 12 g fat, 11 mg chol, 996 mg sodium, 33 g carb, 7 g fiber, 15 g pro.*

BUTTERY POACHED
SHRIMP SALAD

# MATZO MAKEOVER

Michele Heilbrun knows matzo: Her family company has been making the flatbread for more than 90 years. And her new book proves there are dozens of innovative ways to enjoy the Passover staple long after the Seder.

**MATZO CHILAQUILES**
*Recipe on page 90*

**COD CAKES WITH
REMOULADE SAUCE**
*Recipe on page 90*

## MIX 'N' MATCH CHICKEN WINGS

*Choose whole chicken wings for the optimum meat-to-crispy-skin ratio. Whole wings have three parts: the drumette, which is attached to the chicken and shaped like a drumstick; the wingette or flat middle portion of the wing; and the tips.*

**HANDS-ON TIME** 25 min.
**TOTAL TIME** 3 hr. 30 min.

24  whole chicken wings (4 to 5 lb.)
3   cups buttermilk
2   Tbsp. bottled hot sauce
    Wings Rub, right
    Wings Sauce, right

**1.** Place chicken wings, buttermilk, and hot sauce in a large resealable plastic bag set in a shallow dish; seal. Shake to coat wings. Chill 2 to 8 hours. Drain wings; pat dry.
**2.** Place wings in a new large resealable bag. Sprinkle desired Rub over chicken wings; seal. Shake to coat wings. If desired, chill 6 to 24 hours.
**3.** Prepare grill for indirect heat using a drip pan. Place half the wings over drip pan. Grill, covered, over medium heat 30 minutes or until chicken is no longer pink, turning once. Transfer wings to a baking pan lined with aluminum foil. Cover with additional foil. Keep warm in a 300°F oven while grilling remaining wings.
**4.** Toss wings with desired Sauce to coat. Makes 24 wings.

## FLAVOR IT YOUR WAY  Amplify the hint of heat from the buttermilk-hot-sauce marinade with these mix-and-match rubs and sauces.

### HERE'S THE RUB

**CAJUN** Stir together 1 Tbsp. ground black pepper, 1 tsp. crushed dried thyme, 1 tsp. onion powder, 1 tsp. garlic powder, 1 tsp. cayenne pepper, and ½ tsp. salt.

**SAVORY** Stir together 1 Tbsp. garlic salt, 1 Tbsp. crushed dried oregano, 1 Tbsp. cayenne pepper, and 1 Tbsp. black pepper.

**BBQ** Stir together 1 Tbsp. brown sugar, 1 Tbsp. chili powder, 2 tsp. onion powder, 2 tsp. garlic salt, 2 tsp. paprika, 1 tsp. dry mustard powder, and 1 tsp. cayenne pepper.

### GET SAUCY

**CLASSIC BUFFALO** In a small saucepan cook 1 cup cayenne pepper sauce, ½ cup melted butter, ¼ cup white wine vinegar, 1 tsp. Worcestershire sauce, and ½ tsp. garlic powder over medium heat for 5 minutes, stirring constantly.

**SRIRACHA** In a small saucepan cook ½ cup sriracha, ⅓ cup packed brown sugar, 3 Tbsp. soy sauce, and 3 Tbsp. rice wine vinegar over medium heat for 5 minutes, stirring constantly. Remove from heat. Stir in 1 tsp. toasted sesame oil.

**CAJUN SPICE** In a saucepan cook ¼ cup each chopped onion and red sweet pepper in 1 Tbsp. hot oil over medium heat for 4 minutes. Combine ½ cup beer, ½ cup cold water, 1 Tbsp. cornstarch, 1 Tbsp. Cajun seasoning, and ¼ tsp. salt; add to onion mixture. Cook and stir until thickened and bubbly; cook and stir 2 minutes more.

**CHIMICHURRI** In a blender combine ½ cup fresh Italian parsley, ¾ cup fresh cilantro, ½ cup red wine vinegar, ½ cup olive oil, and 4 cloves garlic. Blend until smooth. Transfer to a bowl. Stir in ½ tsp. salt and ½ tsp. crushed red pepper.

# FAST & FRESH

Easy, healthful recipes for a better dinner tonight.

**COBB SALAD
GRILLED CHICKEN**

## COBB SALAD GRILLED CHICKEN

*These suggestions make peeling hard-cooked eggs easier: Start with eggs that have been in the fridge for a week rather than super-fresh ones and transfer eggs to a bowl of ice water immediately after cooking so they contract slightly in their shells.*

**HANDS-ON TIME** 30 min.
**TOTAL TIME** 50 min.

| | |
|---|---|
| 1 | cup chopped red onion |
| 3 | Tbsp. red wine vinegar |
| 1 | tsp. Dijon-style mustard |
| 4 | skinless, boneless chicken breast halves, pounded to ¾-inch thickness |
| 3 | Tbsp. olive oil |
| 2 | hard-cooked eggs, peeled and halved |
| 1 | ripe avocado, halved, pitted, peeled, and sliced |
| 2 | oz. blue cheese |
| 1 | head romaine lettuce, torn (8 to 10 cups) |
| 6 | slices bacon, crisp-cooked and coarsely crumbled |

**1.** In a small bowl stir together onion, vinegar, mustard, and a pinch of salt; let stand at least 30 minutes.
**2.** Meanwhile, season chicken on both sides with salt and black pepper; brush with 1 Tbsp. olive oil. Grill on rack of a covered grill directly over medium-high heat for 8 to 10 minutes or until 165°F, turning once.
**3.** Divide chicken, egg halves, avocado, and blue cheese on romaine among four plates. Whisk remaining 2 Tbsp. olive oil into onion mixture; drizzle over salads. Sprinkle with bacon. Makes 4 servings.
**EACH SERVING** *596 cal, 32 g fat, 281 mg chol, 657 mg sodium, 11 g carb, 5 g fiber, 63 g pro.*

**FRESH PEA AND RICOTTA TARTINE**

## FRESH PEA AND RICOTTA TARTINE

*Whisking the ricotta smooths and fluffs the texture. For added richness, use whole-milk ricotta.*

**HANDS-ON TIME** 25 min.
**TOTAL TIME** 35 min.

| | |
|---|---|
| 1 | 15-oz. carton whole-milk ricotta cheese |
| 1 | lb. mixed fresh peas, such as sugar snap pea pods, snow pea pods, and/or shelled English peas |
| 2 | Tbsp. extra-virgin olive oil |
| ½ | cup thinly sliced shallot |
| 6 | thick slices crusty bread, toasted |
| 1½ | cups pea shoots, pea sprouts, or baby lettuce leaves |
| | Champagne vinegar |
| | Flake sea salt |

**1.** Whisk ricotta in a medium bowl for 30 seconds; season with salt and black pepper. Bring a large pot of salted water to boiling. Add peas. Cook 3 minutes or until bright green and crisp-tender. Drain in a colander; rinse with cold water. Drain well.
**2.** In a small skillet heat oil over medium heat. Add shallot. Cook 7 minutes or until softened and just golden, stirring occasionally. Remove from heat.
**3.** Spread toasted bread slices generously with ricotta. Toss peas and pea shoots together; mound over ricotta. Spoon shallot mixture over all. Drizzle with vinegar. Sprinkle with flake sea salt. Makes 6 servings.
**EACH SERVING** *336 cal, 14 g fat, 36 mg chol, 559 mg sodium, 37 g carb, 5 g fiber, 16 g pro.*

GREENS, EGGS, AND HAM FRITTATA

## ROASTED TOMATO AND ARTICHOKE PASTA

*When you drain the marinated artichoke hearts, don't toss the liquid, which is often a flavorful mix of oil, vinegar, salt, and spices. Use it for a quick vinaigrette, drizzle some over grilled vegetables, or brush on baguette slices to toast in the oven.*

**HANDS-ON TIME** 15 min.
**TOTAL TIME** 25 min.

| | |
|---|---|
| 8 | oz. dried campanelle or penne pasta |
| ¼ | cup extra-virgin olive oil |
| 1 | 6.5- to 7.5-oz. jar quartered marinated artichoke hearts, drained |
| 10 | to 12 oz. red and/or yellow cherry tomatoes |
| ½ | cup pitted Kalamata olives, drained |
| 6 | sprigs fresh thyme |
| 6 | sprigs fresh oregano |
| ½ | tsp. crushed red pepper (optional) |

**1.** Preheat oven to 400°F. Cook pasta according to package directions. Drain; return to pot. Toss with 1 Tbsp. olive oil.
**2.** In a shallow baking pan toss artichoke hearts, tomatoes, and olives with remaining 3 Tbsp. oil, the herbs, and, if desired, crushed red pepper. Roast 5 to 7 minutes or until tomatoes are sizzling and beginning to burst, stirring once. Transfer mixture to pot with pasta; toss to combine. Makes 4 servings.
**EACH SERVING** *403 cal, 21 g fat, 0 mg chol, 876 mg sodium, 47 g carb, 3 g fiber, 8 g pro.*

## GREENS, EGGS, AND HAM FRITTATA

*Spring onions look similar to green onions but have a larger bulb that varies from white to purple and tends to be milder and sweeter. The onions are interchangeable in recipes.*

**HANDS-ON TIME** 20 min.
**TOTAL TIME** 50 min.

| | |
|---|---|
| 10 | large eggs |
| 1½ | cups shredded Monterey Jack cheese |
| ½ | cup finely grated Pecorino Romano or Parmesan cheese |
| 4 | to 6 thin slices smoked ham, torn into pieces |
| 2 | Tbsp. butter |
| 2 | Tbsp. olive oil |
| 1 | large spring onion or 4 green onions, sliced into thin rounds |
| 10 | oz. mixed baby greens, such as chard, kale, and/or spinach |

**1.** Preheat oven to 350°F. In a large bowl whisk together eggs, cheeses, ham, and ¼ tsp. black pepper. In an oven-going 10-inch skillet heat 1 Tbsp. butter and 1 Tbsp. oil over medium heat until butter is melted. Add onion; cook and stir 2 minutes or until tender. Gradually add greens; cook and toss 2 minutes or until wilted. Transfer to a colander to drain; press out excess liquid. Stir greens into egg mixture
**2.** In the same skillet heat remaining butter and oil over medium heat until butter is melted. Pour in egg mixture. Bake 20 minutes or until slightly puffed and set. Remove; let cool 10 minutes before serving. Makes 6 servings.
**EACH SERVING** *342 cal, 27 g fat, 356 mg chol, 498 mg sodium, 3 g carb, 1 g fiber, 21 g pro.*

ROASTED TOMATO
AND ARTICHOKE
PASTA

FISH WITH CRISPY
BREAD CRUMBS,
SPINACH, AND ONIONS

## FISH WITH CRISPY BREAD CRUMBS, SPINACH, AND ONIONS

*Vidalia and Walla Walla onions, prized for their sweet flavor, are named for the cities in which they're grown in Georgia and Washington, respectively. Both are available nationwide during summer.*

**TOTAL TIME** 30 min.

4   fresh or frozen skinless flounder, tilapia, or cod fillets, ½ inch thick
2   lemons
1   cup coarse soft bread crumbs
1   Tbsp. chopped fresh tarragon
¼   cup butter
1   Tbsp. olive oil
2   Vidalia or Walla Walla onions (1¼ lb. total), halved and sliced (4 cups)
1   5- to 6-oz. pkg. baby spinach

1. Thaw fish, if frozen. Pat dry with paper towels. Season with salt and pepper. Slice one lemon; halve other lemon. In a medium bowl toss bread crumbs with tarragon and a pinch of salt. In an extra-large skillet heat 1 Tbsp. butter over medium heat. Add crumb mixture. Cook and stir 4 to 5 minutes or until toasted. Remove from skillet.

2. In the same skillet heat 2 Tbsp. butter and the olive oil over medium heat. Add onions and a pinch of salt. Cook and stir 10 minutes or until tender but not brown. Add lemon slices and spinach; toss until spinach is lightly wilted. Remove from skillet.

3. Heat remaining 1 Tbsp. butter in the skillet over medium heat. Add fish. Cook 4 to 6 minutes or until fish flakes easily with a fork, turning once. Transfer to four plates; top with crumb mixture. Serve with spinach mixture. Squeeze lemon halves over each serving. Makes 4 servings.

**EACH SERVING** *396 cal, 18 g fat, 112 mg chol, 436 mg sodium, 25 g carb, 5 g fiber, 36 g pro.*

# *new ways with*
# CARROTS

This thin-skinned gem knows more than one way to make a splash at summer potlucks.

They may be a crisper-drawer staple year-round, but late spring and early summer are the best times to find local and organic carrots at their prime at farmers markets. Very large carrots tend to be less sweet than their slender ones, so look for young, thin-skinned roots that are 1-inch diameter or less. They should be bright, firm, and free of cracks. And if they're fresh, peeling isn't necessary. Give them a scrub and a rinse, and you're all set.

INDIVIDUAL
MASHED CARROT
AND POTATO BAKES

ROASTED CARROTS
WITH CARROT-TOP
PESTO

ROSEMARY AND
CARROT RIBBON
PAPPARDELLE

THE SUBTLE TASTE AMONG ORANGE, WHITE, RED, AND PURPLE CARROTS IS MORE EVIDENT WHEN YOU EAT THE CARROTS RAW—SO MIX IT UP!

### ROSEMARY AND CARROT RIBBON PAPPARDELLE

**TOTAL TIME** 30 min.

1    lb. carrots, peeled
8    oz. dried pappardelle
½    cup chopped, toasted* hazelnuts
2    Tbsp. butter
2    Tbsp. chopped fresh rosemary
½    tsp. kosher salt
4    oz. goat cheese, cut up

**1.** Using a vegetable peeler, cut carrots into flat ribbons. Transfer to a large colander.
**2.** Meanwhile cook pappardelle in lightly salted boiling water according to package directions. Drain in same colander as carrots, reserving 1 cup cooking liquid.
**3.** In a large skillet heat hazelnuts, butter, fresh rosemary, and salt over medium heat until bubbling. Add ½ cup reserved pasta water and goat cheese, whisking until combined. Add pasta and carrot mixture, tossing gently to coat. Add reserved cooking liquid to thin sauce as desired. Sprinkle with additional chopped toasted hazelnuts. Makes 4 servings.
**\* Tip** To toast hazelnuts, preheat oven to 350°F. Spread nuts in a shallow baking pan. Bake 8 to 10 minutes or until nuts are lightly toasted. Cool nuts slightly; place on a clean kitchen towel. Rub nuts with towel to remove loose skins.
**EACH SERVING** *508 cal, 26 g fat, 45 mg chol, 453 mg sodium, 52 g carb, 5 g fiber, 19 g pro.*

### ROASTED CARROTS WITH CARROT-TOP PESTO

**HANDS-ON TIME** 20 min.
**TOTAL TIME** 45 min.

3    bunches rainbow carrots with tops (about 2 lb. total with tops)
2    cups loosely packed basil leaves
⅓    cup grated Parmesan cheese
¼    cup toasted* pine nuts
4    cloves garlic, halved
¼    tsp. kosher salt
⅓    cup olive oil

**1.** Preheat oven to 425°F. Trim tops from carrots; thoroughly rinse and dry. Strip the leaves from the stems and measure 2 cups loosely packed leaves; discard stems. Place carrot tops in a food processor with the basil, cheese, pine nuts, garlic, and kosher salt. With food processor running, drizzle in the ⅓ cup oil in a stream until pureed and smooth, scraping sides as needed; set aside.
**2.** Peel carrots. In a 15×10×1-inch baking pan toss carrots with 2 Tbsp. olive oil and ½ tsp. each regular salt and black pepper. Roast for 25 minutes or until tender. Top roasted carrots with pesto. Store any remaining pesto in an airtight container in the refrigerator up to 1 week. Makes 4 servings.
**\* Tip** To toast nuts, preheat oven to 350°F. Spread nuts in a shallow baking pan. Bake 5 to 10 minutes or until nuts are light brown, shaking pan once or twice.
**EACH SERVING** *385 cal, 33 g fat, 6 mg chol, 651 mg sodium, 20 g carb, 6 g fiber, 6 g pro.*

### INDIVIDUAL MASHED CARROT AND POTATO BAKES

**HANDS-ON TIME** 20 min.
**TOTAL TIME** 1 hr. 25 min.

1    lb. carrots, peeled and cut into 2-inch chunks
1    lb. potatoes, peeled and cut into 2-inch chunks
½    cup heavy cream
1    cup shredded white cheddar cheese (4 oz.)
1    egg, lightly beaten
½    tsp. kosher salt
     Toasted rye or pumpernickel bread

**1.** Preheat oven to 425°F. In a 4-quart pot cook carrots and potatoes in lightly salted water for 25 to 30 minutes or until very tender. Drain. Let stand 10 minutes to cool slightly.
**2.** Transfer to a large bowl; coarsely mash. Stir in cream, cheese, egg, and salt.
**3.** Divide mixture among four 8- to 10-oz. ramekins. Bake for 25 minutes or until lightly browned. Serve with toasted rye bread. Makes 4 servings.
**EACH SERVING** *437 cal, 23 g fat, 110 mg chol, 735 mg sodium, 45 g carb, 8 g fiber, 15 g pro.*

# POP ART

Put your go-to summertime refreshments on ice along with fresh fruits and herbs. Ice tea, coconut water, and almond milk in colorful ice pops.

**KIWI-STRAWBERRY ICE TEA POPS**
*Recipe on page 142*

# july

Upgrade your summer fare with artsy fruit pops, patio-worthy drinks, and oven-free entrées. Find mouthwatering recipes for peaches and experiment with new dishes that feature okra.

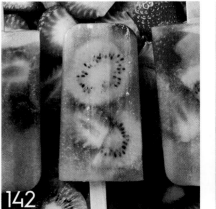

142

155

163

RIBEYE STEAKS
AND PEACHES
Recipe on page 148

## CHERRY HONEYCOMB COBBLER

*Photo on page 134.*

**HANDS-ON TIME** 30 min.
**TOTAL TIME** 1 hr. 20 min.

### HONEYCOMB COOKIES

2    cups all-purpose flour
⅔    cup sugar
1    Tbsp. chopped fresh thyme
1    tsp. salt
¾    cup cold unsalted butter (1½ sticks), cut into pieces
3    Tbsp. honey

### BAKED CHERRIES

1    Tbsp. chopped fresh thyme
¼    cup honey
2    Tbsp. cornstarch
1    orange (2 tsp. zest, ¼ cup juice)
9    cups fresh tart red cherries, pitted, or three 16-oz. pkg. frozen pitted tart red cherries, thawed and drained (about 6 to 7 cups)

### TOPPING

Vanilla ice cream
Honey
Thyme

**1.** For honeycomb cookies, preheat oven to 325°F. In a large bowl combine flour, sugar, thyme, and salt. Using a pastry blender or your fingertips, cut or rub in butter until mixture resembles coarse crumbs. Using a fork, stir in honey. Gently knead in bowl until dough holds together.
**2.** On a lightly floured surface roll dough to ¼-inch thickness. Cut dough using a 2-inch hexagon-shape cutter. Place cutouts 1 inch apart on two ungreased cookie sheets. Reroll scraps.
**3.** Bake 13 to 15 minutes or until edges are firm and tops are lightly browned. Transfer to a wire rack; cool.
**4.** For baked cherries, increase oven to 400°F. In a 2-quart baking dish stir together thyme, honey, cornstarch, zest, and juice. Stir in 4 cups cherries. Bake 25 minutes or until thickened and bubbly; remove from oven. Stir in remaining cherries; cool slightly. Top with honeycomb cookies in a honeycomb pattern; serve remaining cookies on the side. Top cobbler with vanilla ice cream, honey, and thyme. Makes 6 to 8 servings.

**EACH SERVING** *733 cal, 28 g fat, 77 mg chol, 228 mg sodium, 118 g carb, 5 g fiber, 8 g pro.*

## STRAWBERRY MERINGUE COOKIES

*Photo on page 135.*

*Make these cookies on the large side—you'll want more than a couple bites of this delicate meringue laced with strawberry puree. Tuck them into a picnic basket as is, crumble them over a scoop of chocolate ice cream, or use them as bookends for ice cream sandwiches.*

**HANDS-ON TIME** 20 min.
**TOTAL TIME** 3 hr. 5 min.

6    egg whites
1½    cups fresh strawberries, hulled
½    tsp. cream of tartar
½    tsp. vanilla
1⅓    cups sugar

**1.** Allow egg whites to stand at room temperature 30 minutes. Meanwhile, line two baking sheets with parchment paper. Draw six 3½-inch circles on each paper. Flip paper over; set sheets aside.
**2.** In a blender or food processor puree strawberries; set aside.
**3.** Preheat oven to 250°F. In a large mixing bowl beat egg whites, cream of tartar, vanilla, and a pinch of salt with a mixer on medium until soft peaks form. Add sugar, 1 Tbsp. at a time, beating on high until stiff, glossy peaks form (5 minutes).
**4.** Mound about two-thirds of the egg white mixture onto circles on parchment; spoon puree over mounds. Top with remaining meringue. Using the back of a spoon, lightly spread to edge of circle. Bake 75 minutes with sheets on separate oven racks. Turn off oven. Prop open oven door with a wooden spoon; let sheets sit in oven 1 hour. Transfer with paper to wire racks; cool completely. Store in an airtight container; refrigerate up to 3 days. Makes 12 cookies.

**EACH SERVING** *102 cal, 40 mg sodium, 24 g carb, 2 g pro.*

## RASPBERRY ANGEL CUPCAKES

**HANDS-ON TIME** 40 min.
**TOTAL TIME** 2 hr.

### ANGEL CUPCAKES

1½    cups egg whites (10 to 12 large eggs)
1½    cups powdered sugar
1    cup all-purpose flour
1½    tsp. cream of tartar
1    tsp. vanilla
1    cup granulated sugar
1    cup fresh raspberries

### MARSHMALLOW FROSTING

1½    cups unsalted butter (3 sticks), cut into 1-inch pieces, softened
2    7-oz. jars marshmallow creme
½    cup powdered sugar
1    tsp. vanilla

### TOPPING

Fresh raspberries and blueberries
Powdered sugar

**1.** For cupcakes, in an extra-large mixing bowl let egg whites stand at room temperature 30 minutes. Meanwhile, sift powdered sugar and flour together three times; set aside.
**2.** Preheat oven to 350°F. Line 3½-inch muffin cups with paper bake cups.
**3.** Add cream of tartar and vanilla to egg whites. Using a mixer on medium, beat until soft peaks form. Add granulated sugar, 2 Tbsp. at a time, beating until stiff peaks form.
**4.** Sift one-fourth of the flour mixture over egg whites; fold in gently. Repeat, folding in remaining flour mixture by fourths. Spoon into bake cups, filling each to top of cup. Bake 20 minutes or until tops are lightly browned and spring back when lightly touched. Transfer pan to a wire rack; cool 5 minutes. Remove bake cups from pan; cool completely.
**5.** Using the handle of a wooden spoon, poke a hole in the center and to the bottom of each cupcake. Fill centers with 3 or 4 berries.
**6.** For marshmallow frosting, in a large mixing bowl beat softened butter with a mixer on medium until light and fluffy. Add marshmallow creme; beat until smooth, scraping sides of bowl. Add powdered sugar, vanilla, and 1 tsp. salt; beat until light and fluffy. (If frosting is too stiff to spread, soften in a microwave oven no more than 10 seconds; beat again until smooth.) Using a pastry bag fitted with a large round tip, pipe frosting. Hold pastry bag directly over each cupcake. Squeeze and release, lifting bag; repeat twice. Top with fresh berries and sift with powdered sugar. Makes 12 servings.

**EACH SERVING** *542 cal, 23 g fat, 61 mg chol, 263 mg sodium, 79 g carb, 1 g fiber, 5 g pro.*

GINGER PORK
WITH SWEET
PEPPERS

**PASTA WITH NO-COOK TOMATO SAUCE AND MOZZARELLA**

## PASTA WITH NO-COOK TOMATO SAUCE AND MOZZARELLA

*No need to cook tomatoes when you want fresh sauce. Simply combine them with a few glugs of your best olive oil, garlic, salt, and a ladle or two of pasta cooking liquid. Any variety of ripe tomato works: heirloom, roma, cherry, beefsteak.*

**HANDS-ON TIME** 20 min.
**TOTAL TIME** 40 min.

6   **Tbsp. olive oil**
4   **garlic cloves, thinly sliced**
2   **lb. tomatoes, cored and cut into chunks**
1   **lb. dried rigatoni**
½   **lb. small fresh mozzarella balls**
1   **cup torn or sliced fresh basil leaves**
⅓   **cup chopped fresh chives**

**1.** In an extra-large bowl combine oil and garlic. Add tomatoes and 1 tsp. salt; toss to coat.
**2.** Cook pasta according to package directions. Drain, reserving ½ cup cooking liquid. Add pasta and ¼ cup cooking liquid to tomato mixture; toss to combine. Stir in mozzarella. Cover bowl; let stand 10 minutes.
**3.** Add basil, chives, black pepper, and a drizzle of additional olive oil to pasta mixture. Add remaining pasta water as needed to reach desired sauciness. Serve at room temperature. Makes 4 servings.
**EACH SERVING** *532 cal, 24 g fat, 27 mg chol, 309 mg sodium, 63 g carb, 5 g fiber, 18 g pro.*

# *new ways with*
# OKRA

If you love okra in gumbo but not much else, these recipes will broaden your taste.

The pods' reputation as slimy comes from mucilage (a protein-based substance also found in aloe vera and quinces) around the seeds, which becomes gelatinous when heated, thus making the veggie a good thickener for stews. Hot and fast cooking—grilling, frying, roasting—reduces the slippery texture.

FRIED OKRA
SALAD

SHEET PAN
SUCCOTASH

GRILLED OKRA
TACOS

FIND OKRA (INCLUDING PURPLE VARIETIES) AT ITS SEASONAL PEAK MAY THROUGH OCTOBER. LARGE PODS CAN BE TOUGH AND FIBROUS, SO CHOOSE THOSE LESS THAN 4 INCHES LONG.

## GRILLED OKRA TACOS

**TOTAL TIME** 30 min.

- 2 cups fresh raspberries and/or blueberries
- ½ cup salsa
- 1 Tbsp. chili powder
- 1½ tsp. ground cumin
- ½ tsp. ground coriander
- ½ tsp. kosher salt
- 1 lb. fresh okra (halve any large pods)
- 2 Tbsp. extra-virgin olive oil
- 16 6-inch corn tortillas, warmed*
- ½ cup sour cream
- 2 oz. queso fresco or feta cheese, crumbled (½ cup)

**1.** For berry salsa, in a medium bowl combine raspberries and salsa.
**2.** In a large bowl combine chili powder, cumin, coriander, and salt. Add okra and olive oil; toss to coat. Thread okra onto six sets of two parallel 10-inch skewers**, leaving ¼ inch between each piece. Grill, covered, over medium-high heat for 5 minutes or until charred and crisp-tender, turning once. Remove okra from skewers.
**3.** Serve in corn tortillas with berry salsa, sour cream, and queso fresco. Makes 4 servings.
**\*Tip** Place tortillas between paper towels. Microwave on high for 20 to 30 seconds. Or wrap in foil and place on the grill. Heat for 5 minutes, turning packet once.
**\*\*Tip** When using wood skewers, soak them in water at least 30 minutes before threading on food.
**EACH SERVING** *437 cal, 19 g fat, 24 mg chol, 667 mg sodium, 61 g carb, 15 g fiber, 11 g pro.*

## SHEET PAN SUCCOTASH

**TOTAL TIME** 30 min.

- 12 oz. okra, halved lengthwise
- 2 orange, yellow, and/or red sweet peppers, cut into 1½-inch pieces
- 1 10- to 12-oz. pkg. frozen shelled edamame
- ¼ cup extra-virgin olive oil
- 16 oz. cherry tomatoes, halved
- ¼ cup chopped fresh dill weed
- 2 Tbsp. apple cider vinegar

**1.** Heat a 15×10×1-inch pan in a 450°F oven for 10 minutes. Meanwhile, in a large bowl combine okra, sweet peppers, edamame, olive oil, and 1 tsp. salt. Transfer to the heated pan.
**2.** Roast 20 to 25 minutes or just until tender, adding cherry tomatoes the last 5 minutes. Remove from oven. Stir in dill weed and vinegar. Makes 8 servings.
**EACH SERVING** *140 cal, 9 g fat, 300 mg sodium, 12 g carb, 4 g fiber, 6 g pro.*

## FRIED OKRA SALAD

**TOTAL TIME** 40 min.

- ⅓ cup mayonnaise
- 1¾ cups buttermilk
- 1 Tbsp. lemon juice
- ⅓ cup crumbled blue cheese
  Kosher salt
  Black pepper
  Vegetable oil
- 6 oz. fresh okra, trimmed and cut into ½-inch pieces
- 6 green onions, trimmed and halved crosswise
- 2 jalapeño peppers, quartered lengthwise and seeded (tip page 102)
- ¾ cup all-purpose flour
- ¾ cup cornmeal
- 1 head Bibb lettuce, torn

**1.** For dressing, in a small bowl stir together mayonnaise, ¼ cup buttermilk, and lemon juice. Stir in blue cheese. Season to taste with kosher salt and black pepper.
**2.** In a Dutch oven heat 2 inches vegetable oil to 350°F. In a medium bowl combine remaining 1½ cups buttermilk, okra, green onions, jalapeños. In a resealable plastic bag combine flour, cornmeal, and ½ tsp. kosher salt.
**3.** Remove one-fourth of the okra from buttermilk mixture, shaking gently to remove excess. Add okra to flour mixture; seal. Shake to coat.
**4.** Fry coated okra in hot oil for 3 to 5 minutes or until golden brown. Remove with a slotted spoon to paper towels. Repeat with remaining okra. Serve with lettuce and dressing.
**EACH SERVING** *580 cal, 45 g fat, 19 mg chol, 617 mg sodium, 36 g carb., 4 g fiber, 9 g pro.*

# *viva* ZUCCHINI

If you need fresh ideas for the bag of zucchini left on your doorstep by well-meaning neighbors, take a virtual trip to Italy, where cooks revere the prolific and accommodating vegetable and make it the star of summer meals. Bring those flavors home with these seven recipes, including creamy baked Parmigiana and tender lemony snacking cake—the perfect thank-you for your generous neighbor.

## GRILLED ZUCCHINI PARMIGIANA

**HANDS-ON TIME** 1 hr.
**TOTAL TIME** 2 hr.

5   very large zucchini (about 4 lb.), ends trimmed and cut lengthwise into ½-inch-thick slices*
¼   cup unsalted butter
1   small spring onion or white onion, finely chopped (⅓ cup)
3   Tbsp. all-purpose flour
2   cups whole milk or reduced-fat milk
2   Tbsp. finely chopped fresh basil, plus more for topping
⅛   tsp. freshly grated nutmeg
8   oz. thinly sliced fresh mozzarella cheese
1   cup freshly grated Parmesan cheese (2 oz.)
    Flake sea salt

**1.** Lightly coat zucchini slices with cooking spray on one side; season with ½ tsp. salt and ¼ tsp. black pepper. Working in batches, grill zucchini on the rack of a covered grill over high heat on coated side for 4 to 8 minutes or until char marks form; remove. Set aside. Preheat oven to 375°F. Butter a 9×13-inch baking dish.

**2.** For white sauce, in a medium saucepan melt butter and cook onion over medium heat for 5 minutes or until softened. Add flour; cook 3 minutes or until light golden brown, stirring constantly. Add milk, whisking to combine well; bring to boiling. Reduce heat; simmer 2 minutes, stirring often. Stir in basil, nutmeg, ½ tsp. salt, and ¼ tsp. black pepper. Remove from heat.

**3.** Layer a third of white sauce, a third of zucchini slices (grill marks up), and half each of mozzarella and Parmesan; repeat layers. Top with remaining sauce and zucchini slices (grill marks up).

**4.** Bake, uncovered, 30 to 40 minutes or until bubbling and nicely browned. Remove; let stand 20 minutes. Top with additional fresh basil and flake sea salt. Makes 6 to 8 servings.

***Tip** Ideally, choose zucchini about 9 inches long to cover the width of the baking dish.

**EACH SERVING** *338 cal, 22 g fat, 67 mg chol, 981 mg sodium, 19 g carb, 3 g fiber, 17 g pro.*

## A CUT ABOVE

**SPIRALIZING** The various blades of a spiralizer determine thickness. This noodle holds its shape without becoming limp.

**SLICING** A mandoline guarantees the same thickness for every slice. Try ⅛-inch slices for pickling; they're thin enough to absorb brine and thick enough to maintain crunch.

**CORING** Use an apple corer at each end to reach the center of a medium zucchini.

LAYERING SLABS OF GRILLED ZUCCHINI WITH MOZZARELLA AND PARMESAN AND BASIL-INFUSED BÉCHAMEL? THAT'S AMORE!

TAKE SPIRAL-CUT ZUCCHINI FROM DIET DARLING TO DINNER-PARTY FARE BY TOSSING IT WITH AL DENTE SPAGHETTI AND A SAFFRON-SPIKED SAUCE. THE CRISP NOTES OF AN ITALIAN PINOT GRIGIO BALANCE THE CREAMY NOTES.

**NOODLES AND "ZOODLES" WITH SAFFRON AND CREAM**
*Recipe on page 185*

**SKILLET ZUCCHINI**
*Recipe on page 185*

MEATBALLS
AND STUFFED
ZUCCHINI

JAMBALAYA EGG
BAKE

TWO-BITE BANH MI TOASTS WITH FRIED GREEN TOMATOES MASH UP SOUTHERN AND VIETNAMESE FLAVORS—BOTH PREVALENT IN NEW ORLEANS.

**FRIED GREEN TOMATO BANH MI TOASTS**
*Recipe on page 200*

**DIRTY RICE-
STUFFED
TOMATOES**
*Recipe on page 205*

WILTED
MUSTARD
GREENS

# RISE. EAT. SHINE.

Cookies and bars for breakfast? Absolutely! These recipes are perfect for making and freezing so you never have an excuse to skip the most important meal of the day—even in the morning rush.

BREAKFAST
FRUIT-AND-NUT
COOKIES

## BREAKFAST FRUIT-AND-NUT COOKIES

*The combination of ingredients in this cookie provides complex carbs, good fats, and protein to supply a steady stream of fuel. Oat bran is the complex carb that keeps blood sugar and energy stable. Pecans and flaxseeds have good fats; dates or figs supply protein plus iron and calcium.*

**HANDS-ON TIME** 25 min.
**TOTAL TIME** 36 min.

4  eggs, lightly beaten
1⅓  cups packed brown sugar
6  Tbsp. butter, melted
2  tsp. vanilla
½  cup finely snipped dried dates or golden figs
2  cups all-purpose flour
1  cup whole wheat flour
½  cup oat bran
¼  cup flaxseed meal
1  tsp. baking soda
1  tsp. ground cinnamon
½  cup chopped toasted* pecans

**1.** Preheat oven to 350°F. Line two cookie sheets with parchment paper. In a large bowl combine eggs, brown sugar, butter, and vanilla. Stir in dates.
**2.** In a medium bowl combine the next six ingredients (through cinnamon). Add flour mixture to date mixture, stirring until moist. Stir in pecans. Using a scant ¼-cup measure or scoop, drop dough into mounds about 3 inches apart onto prepared cookie sheets.
**3.** Bake 10 to 12 minutes or until edges are golden. Cool on cookie sheets 1 minute. Remove; cool cookies on a wire rack. Makes 20 cookies.
**\* Tip** To toast nuts, preheat oven to 350°F. Spread nuts in a shallow baking pan. Bake 5 to 10 minutes or until nuts are light brown, shaking pan once or twice.
**To Store** Layer cookies between sheets of waxed paper in an airtight container; cover. Store at room temperature up to 2 days or freeze up to 3 months.
**EACH COOKIE** *211 cal, 7 g fat, 46 mg chol, 109 mg sodium, 34 g carb, 2 g fiber, 4 g pro.*

## CHOCOLATE MONKEY BARS

*Photo on page 210.*

*Peanut butter with magnesium, potassium, and healthy fats amps up the staying power and nutritional profile of these bars. Another unsung superfood, unsweetened cocoa powder, contributes antioxidants and flavor.*

**HANDS-ON TIME** 20 min.
**TOTAL TIME** 1 hr. 20 min.

   Nonstick cooking spray
¾  cup crunchy peanut butter
½  cup honey
3  Tbsp. coconut oil
2  Tbsp. unsweetened cocoa powder
2  cups regular rolled oats, toasted*
2  cups banana nut granola
2  cups whole grain wheat and brown rice cereal flakes, such as Total
½  cup roasted, salted pepitas

**1.** Line a 9×13-inch baking pan with foil, extending foil over edges of pan. Coat foil with cooking spray.
**2.** In a 4- to 6-quart pot combine the next four ingredients (through cocoa powder). Stir over medium heat until melted and nearly smooth. Remove from heat. Stir in the remaining ingredients.
**3.** Spoon mixture into the prepared baking pan; press firmly. Cover with waxed paper, set another pan inside, and weight mixture down with cans of food. Chill 1 to 2 hours or until firm enough to cut. Remove cans and pan. Using foil, lift uncut bars from pan. Cut into bars. Makes 24 bars.
**\*Tip** To toast oats, preheat oven to 350°F. Spread oats in a shallow baking pan. Bake 10 to 15 minutes or until golden, stirring twice.
**To Store** Layer bars between sheets of waxed paper in an airtight container; cover. Refrigerate up to 1 week or freeze up to 3 months.
**EACH BAR** *195 cal, 11 g fat, 74 mg sodium, 22 g carb, 3 g fiber, 6 g pro.*

## ORANGE-ALMOND BREAKFAST BARS

*Photo on page 211.*

*Almonds and dried fruit are a head start on fiber, calcium, and iron intake for the day. Almonds have the highest amount of calcium of any nut, with 75 milligrams in 1 ounce; a serving of dried apricots contains 20 percent of daily fiber needs, plus iron, which is easier to absorb when combined with the vitamin C in oranges.*

**HANDS-ON TIME** 20 min.
**TOTAL TIME** 32 min.

   Nonstick cooking spray
1  large orange
¼  cup packed brown sugar
1  cup chopped pitted whole dried dates and/or dried apricots
1¼  cups all-purpose flour
1¼  cups whole wheat flour
½  tsp. baking soda
¼  tsp. baking powder
¼  tsp. salt
1  egg, lightly beaten
⅓  cup honey
¼  cup almond butter
1  cup chopped almonds

**1.** Preheat oven to 350°F. Line a 9×13-inch baking pan with foil, extending foil over edges of pan. Lightly coat foil with cooking spray.
**2.** Remove 1 tsp. zest and squeeze ½ cup juice from orange. In a bowl combine zest, juice, and brown sugar. Stir in dates and/or apricots.
**3.** In a large bowl stir together the next five ingredients (through salt). Add egg, honey, and almond butter; whisk to combine. Add to flour mixture Stir in almonds. Spoon into the prepared pan. Use moistened hands to pat dough in pan.
**4.** Bake 12 minutes or until edges are browned and a toothpick inserted in center comes out clean. Cool in pan on a wire rack. Cut into bars. Makes 16 bars.
**To Store** Layer cookies between sheets of waxed paper in an airtight container; cover. Store at room temperature up to 2 days or freeze up to 3 months.
**EACH BAR** *205 cal, 6 g fat, 12 mg chol, 99 mg sodium, 35 g carb, 3 g fiber, 5 g pro.*

COD AND
TOMATOES WITH
CRISPY PARSLEY
CRUMBS

# *day of the dead:*
# IN GOOD SPIRITS

Día de los Muertos, the traditional Mexican holiday that honors the spiritual journey of deceased family and friends, is commemorated even north of the border.

RASPBERRY OR MANGO SPRITZ-ADE COCKTAILS

## RASPBERRY SPRITZ-ADE COCKTAILS

**TOTAL TIME** 10 min.

5   cups frozen raspberries or mangoes, thawed
2   cups lemonade
1   cup tequila (optional)
1   12-oz. can sparkling water, chilled
¼   cup agave nectar (optional)
     Citrus wedges, such as lime, orange, or blood orange (when in season)

**1.** In a blender process fruit until smooth. Strain through a fine-mesh sieve; discard seeds.
**2.** In a pitcher combine puree and lemonade. Add tequila, if desired, and sparkling water. If using raspberries, add agave nectar. Thread citrus wedges onto skewers. Serve over ice. Makes 6 cups (nonalcoholic version).
**PER 6 OZ.** *96 cal, 1 g fat, 10 mg sodium, 24 g carb, 7 g fiber, 2 g pro.*

## ROASTED GARLIC SPREAD

**HANDS-ON TIME** 10 min.
**TOTAL TIME** 50 min.

1   large head garlic
3   Tbsp. plus 1 tsp. olive oil, plus more for drizzling
2   15-oz. cans cannellini beans, rinsed and drained
3   Tbsp. lemon juice
     Roasted, salted pepitas
     Chopped carrot

**1.** To roast garlic, preheat oven to 400°F. Cut off top of garlic head, bulb intact with cloves exposed. Remove any loose skin. Place garlic head, cut side up, in a ramekin or foil. Drizzle with 1 tsp. oil. Cover; bake 25 to 30 minutes or until soft. Let cool.
**2.** Squeeze garlic into a food processor or blender; add remaining 3 Tbsp. oil, the beans, lemon juice, and ½ tsp. salt. Cover; process until smooth. Transfer to a serving bowl. To serve, drizzle with additional olive oil; sprinkle with pepitas and chopped carrot. May be chilled 24 hours. Makes 2¼ cups.
**PER 2 TBSP.** *75 cal, 4 g fat, 148 mg sodium, 7 g carb, 2 g fiber, 3 g pro.*

## SWEET PEA SPREAD

**TOTAL TIME** 15 min.

2   15-oz. cans cannellini beans, rinsed and drained
1   cup frozen shelled peas, thawed
3   Tbsp. olive oil, plus more for drizzling
2   Tbsp. lemon juice
1   tsp. ground cumin
1   clove garlic, peeled
     Flaky sea salt

In a food processor or blender process beans, peas, oil, juice, cumin, garlic, and ½ tsp. salt until smooth. To serve, drizzle with oil; top with flaky sea salt. May be chilled 24 hours. Makes 2¾ cups.
**PER 2 TBSP.** *55 cal, 3 g fat, 138 mg sodium, 6 g carb, 2 g fiber, 2 g pro.*

## PUMPKIN SPREAD

**TOTAL TIME** 20 min.

2   15-oz. cans cannellini beans, rinsed and drained
1   15-oz. can pumpkin
¼   cup orange juice
2   cloves garlic, peeled and halved
2   Tbsp. olive oil, plus more for drizzling
1   tsp. ground cumin
2   tsp. chili powder
     Fresh cilantro leaves

Add beans, pumpkin, orange juice, garlic, oil, cumin, chili powder, and ½ tsp. salt to food processor or blender. Cover; process until nearly smooth. Transfer to a serving bowl. Season to taste with salt. Cover; chill until serving time. To serve, drizzle with additional olive oil and top with cilantro. May be chilled 24 hours. Makes 4 cups.
**PER 2 TBSP.** *33 cal, 1 g fat, 92 mg sodium, 5 g carb, 2 g fiber, 2 g pro.*

## HOMEMADE SALTINES

**HANDS-ON TIME** 20 min.
**TOTAL TIME** 1 hr.

1   cup all-purpose flour
¼   cup water
2   Tbsp. butter, melted
     Smoked salt
     Poppy seeds and/or black sesame seeds

ROASTED GARLIC, SWEET PEA, AND PUMPKIN SPREADS

**1.** In a food processor process flour and ½ tsp. salt. Add the water and melted butter; process until a crumbly dough forms. Transfer to a lightly floured surface; knead until smooth. Cover; let rest 30 minutes.
**2.** Preheat oven to 400°F. Roll dough to ⅛- to 1/16-inch thickness. Cut into 2½-inch rectangles or other desired shape. Arrange on ungreased baking sheet. Prick several times with a fork. Brush with a little water; sprinkle with smoked salt and poppy and/or black sesame seeds. Bake 10 minutes or until golden. Remove; let cool. Store in an airtight container at room temperature up to 3 days. Makes about 24 saltines.
**PER 2 SALTINES** *55 cal, 2 g fat, 5 mg chol, 194 mg sodium, 8 g carb, 1 g pro.*

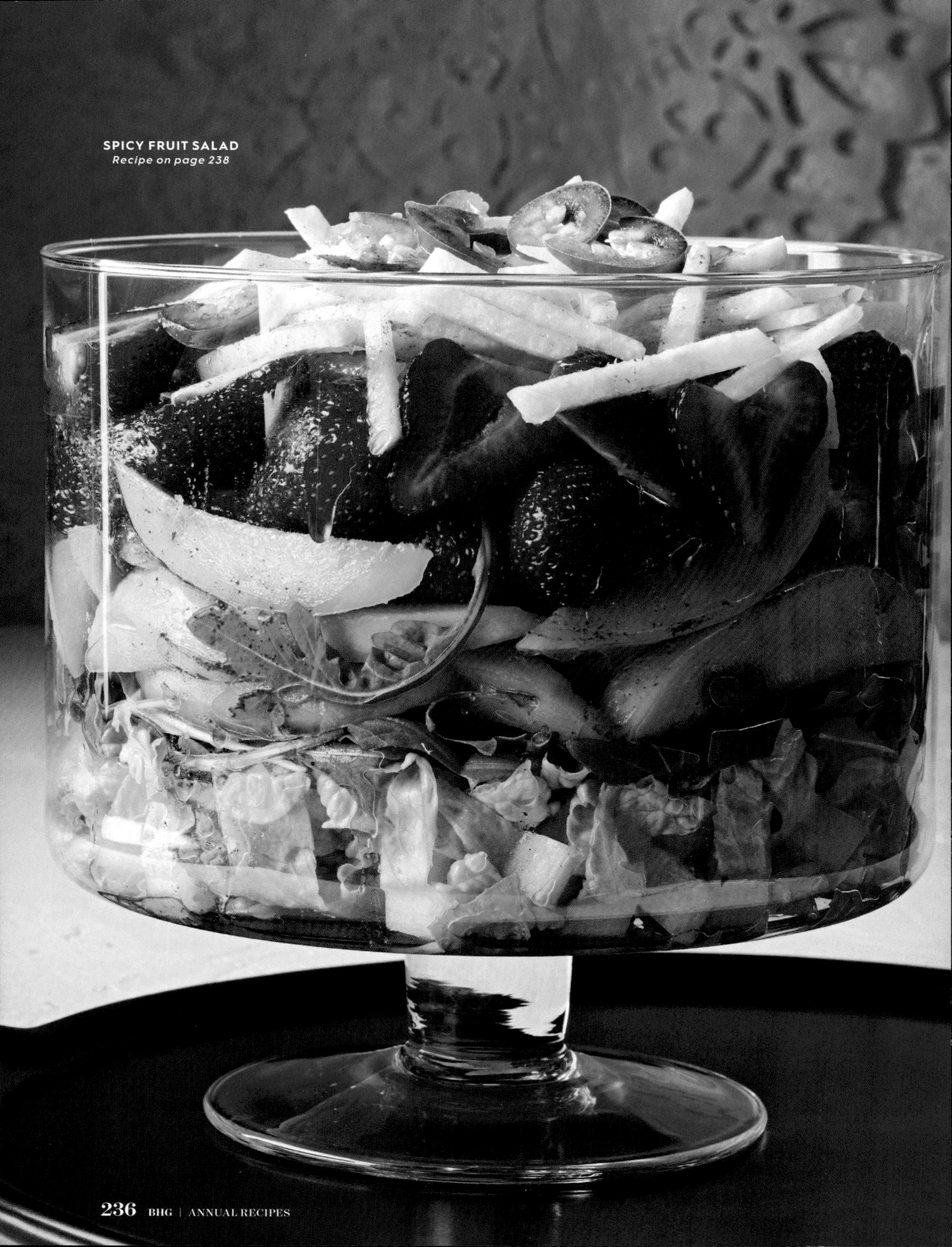

**SPICY FRUIT SALAD**
*Recipe on page 238*

**ENCHILADA CASSEROLE**
*Recipe on page 238*

## SPICY FRUIT SALAD

*Photo on page 236.*

**HANDS ON-TIME** 35 min.
**TOTAL TIME** 4 hr. 35 min.

6    cups shredded romaine lettuce
3    cups arugula
3    mangoes, seeded, peeled, and sliced
3    cups fresh strawberries, halved
1    cup peeled jicama, cut into matchsticks
¼    cup vegetable oil
3    Tbsp. lime juice
1    Tbsp. honey
1    tsp. chili powder
1    tsp. adobo sauce (from a can of chipotles in adobo sauce)
     Sliced jalapeño peppers (tip page 102)

In a 4-quart clear salad or trifle bowl layer romaine, arugula, mangoes, strawberries, and jicama. (May be covered tightly and chilled up to 4 hours.) For dressing, whisk together oil, lime juice, honey, chili powder, adobo sauce, and ¼ tsp. salt. To serve, drizzle dressing over salad; top with jalapeño slices. Makes 16 cups.

**PER 2 CUPS** *149 cal, 8 g fat, 142 mg sodium, 22 g carb, 4 g fiber, 2 g pro.*

## ENCHILADA CASSEROLE

*Photo on page 237.*

*This enchilada twist uses two kinds of soft tortillas—white flour and purple corn—to play up the white-and-black color scheme of its two fillings. For a traditional version, use all corn tortillas (white, yellow, or blue).*

**HANDS-ON TIME** 1 hr. 10 min.
**TOTAL TIME** 2 hr. 15 min.

1    recipe Mexican Rice or four 8.8-oz. pouches cooked Spanish-style rice, heated according to pkg. directions
3    cups chopped cooked chicken
1¼   cups tomatillo salsa (salsa verde)
2    cups shredded Monterey Jack cheese (8 oz.)
2    tsp. ground cumin
4    cloves garlic, minced
2    15-oz. cans black beans
1    Tbsp. vegetable oil
1    cup chopped onion
1    Tbsp. chili powder
6    6-inch white flour tortillas
6    purple corn tortillas*

1    Tbsp. butter
1    Tbsp. all-purpose flour
1    cup whole milk
     Spiralized vegetables, such as beets or carrots (optional)
     Cilantro leaves (optional)

**1.** Preheat oven to 350°F. Grease a 4-quart rectangular baking dish; spread Mexican Rice in bottom; set aside.
**2.** For chicken filling, in a large bowl combine chicken, 1 cup salsa, 1 cup cheese, 1 tsp. cumin, and half the garlic; set aside.
**3.** For black bean filling, drain and rinse one can of beans. Mash second can of beans with liquid. In a large skillet heat oil over medium heat. Add onion and remaining garlic; cook and stir until tender, about 5 minutes. Stir in remaining 1 tsp. cumin and the chili powder. Cook, stirring, 1 minute more. Stir in all the beans.
**4.** Spoon about ½ cup of the chicken filling onto each of the white flour tortillas; roll up. Place filled tortillas, seam sides down, on one side of prepared baking dish. Repeat with bean filling and the purple corn tortillas.
**5.** For cheese sauce, in a small saucepan melt butter over medium heat. Stir in flour until combined; whisk in milk to combine. Cook and stir until thickened and bubbly, about 5 minutes. Whisk in remaining 1 cup cheese until smooth. Stir in remaining ¼ cup salsa. Pour over enchiladas.
**6.** Bake, covered, 30 minutes. Uncover; bake 30 minutes more or until fillings are heated through (165°F). If desired top with spiralized vegetables and cilantro. Makes 12 servings.

**Mexican Rice** In a medium saucepan melt 2 Tbsp. butter over medium heat. Add 1⅓ cups long grain white rice and 2 cloves minced garlic; cook and stir 3 minutes. Stir in 3 cups reduced-sodium chicken broth and 1 tsp. ground turmeric. Bring to boiling; reduce heat. Simmer, covered, 15 minutes or until rice is tender and liquid is absorbed. Stir in 1 cup chopped fresh tomatoes, 1 cup finely chopped green sweet pepper, and ½ cup chopped fresh cilantro.

***Tip** To roll corn tortillas easily, wrap in damp paper towels and microwave 10 seconds or until warm.

**EACH SERVING** *442 cal, 16 g fat, 58 mg chol, 971 mg sodium, 47 g carb, 5 g fiber, 25 g pro.*

## MINI LAYER CAKES

**HANDS-ON TIME** 40 min.
**TOTAL TIME** 1 hr.

6    oz. bittersweet chocolate, chopped
½    cup all-purpose flour
1    tsp. ground cinnamon
1    tsp. hot chili powder
½    tsp. baking powder
¼    tsp. salt
8    Tbsp. butter, at room temperature (1 stick)
½    cup sugar
3    eggs, at room temperature
1    tsp. vanilla
1    recipe Cream Cheese Frosting
     Jelly beans
     Black decorating icing (optional)

**1.** In a small saucepan melt chocolate over low heat; let cool.
**2.** Grease and flour twelve 2½-inch muffin cups. In a small bowl stir together flour, cinnamon, chili powder, baking powder, and salt; set aside.
**3.** Preheat oven to 350°F. In a large mixing bowl beat butter with a mixer on medium to high 30 seconds. Gradually add sugar, beating on medium until combined. Scrape sides of bowl. Beat 2 minutes more. Add eggs, one at a time, beating well after each addition. Beat in melted chocolate and vanilla. Beat in flour mixture just until combined.
**4.** Spoon batter two-thirds full into prepared cups. Bake 15 minutes or until a toothpick inserted in center comes out clean. Cool in cups 5 minutes. Transfer cakes to rack; cool completely.
**5.** Split each cake horizontally. Spread bottom half with Cream Cheese Frosting. Add tops. Spread tops with remaining frosting. Decorate with jelly beans. (If desired, use purchased black decorating icing to pipe dots onto cupcake tops.) Makes 12 cakes.

**Cream Cheese Frosting** In a bowl beat 4 oz. cream cheese, 4 Tbsp. butter (half a stick), and 1 tsp. vanilla on medium until light and fluffy. Gradually beat in 2½ to 3 cups powdered sugar to spreading consistency.

**PER CAKE** *429 cal, 21 g fat, 87 mg chol, 222 mg sodium, 59 g carb, 1 g fiber, 4 g pro.*

MINI LAYER
CAKES

**CHOCOLATE
MIXED NUT PIE**
*Recipe on page 257*

**PUMPKIN BUTTER-
OATMEAL PIE**
*Recipe on page 259*

**APPLE-DOUBLE
CHERRY PIE**
*Recipe on page 258*

# november

Host a potluck or organize a gathering centered on traditional flavors, adding to the celebration with updated recipes and simplified baking.

246 254 268

# FRIENDSGIVING

Think of the Friendsgiving potluck as a breezy, laid-back cousin to the traditional feast. It's a chance to experiment with salads, sides, and desserts, even while the turkey remains the same. And when everyone pitches in, it's less stress for all. Kristin Donnelly, author of *Modern Potluck,* shares her best make-ahead, totable, buffet-friendly recipes and tips for guests and hosts.

**SPICE-ROASTED CARROTS WITH LENTILS**

# SPICE-ROASTED CARROTS WITH LENTILS

**HANDS-ON TIME** 25 min.
**TOTAL TIME** 1 hr.

- 3 lb. baby or small carrots, scrubbed or peeled
- ¼ cup plus 3 Tbsp. extra-virgin olive oil
- 2 tsp. ground coriander
- 2 tsp. ground cumin
- 1 tsp. paprika
  Salt and black pepper
- ½ cup tender fresh herb leaves, such as cilantro, dill, tarragon, mint, and/or basil, coarsely chopped
- ¼ cup finely sliced, pitted Medjool dates, dried figs, or prunes
- 1 lb. dried black beluga lentils or French green lentils
- 1 large onion, quartered lengthwise, peeled, and thinly sliced crosswise
- 1 Tbsp. minced garlic
- ½ tsp. ground cinnamon
- 3 Tbsp. fresh lemon juice
- 1 cup fresh cilantro leaves, coarsely chopped
  Plain yogurt (optional)

**1.** Preheat oven to 425°F. Line two large baking sheets with parchment paper. In a large bowl toss carrots with 3 Tbsp. olive oil, 1 tsp. coriander, 1 tsp. cumin, and the paprika. Season generously with salt and black pepper. Spread carrots on baking sheets.
**2.** Roast 20 to 30 minutes or until carrots are browned and tender, rotating baking sheets and shaking carrots halfway through. Cool slightly. Transfer to a large bowl; toss with herbs and dates.
**3.** Meanwhile, in a medium saucepan cover lentils with water by 2 inches; bring to boiling. Simmer, uncovered, over medium heat until tender, 20 to 25 minutes. Drain, reserving ½ cup cooking liquid; season lentils with salt.
**4.** In a deep skillet heat ¼ cup oil over medium heat. Add onion; season generously with salt. Cook, stirring frequently, until lightly browned, about 15 minutes. Add garlic, remaining coriander and cumin, and the cinnamon;

cook until fragrant, about 1 minute. Add lentils and reserved cooking liquid. Cook until heated through, 2 to 3 minutes. Stir in lemon juice and cilantro.
**5.** Arrange lentils on a platter. Top with carrots. If desired, top with additional herbs and a dollop of yogurt. Serve warm or at room temperature. Makes 12 to 16 servings.
**EACH SERVING** *276 cal, 9 g fat, 485 mg sodium, 41 g carb, 8 g fiber, 11 g pro.*

# PUMPKIN BISCUITS

*Photo on page 244.*

**TOTAL TIME** 35 min.

- 2¼ cups white whole wheat flour, plus more for dusting
- 2 Tbsp. maple sugar or packed light brown sugar
- 1 Tbsp. baking powder
- 1 tsp. kosher salt
- ½ cup unsalted butter, cubed (1 stick)
- 1 cup canned pumpkin puree
- ¾ cup buttermilk
- 1 Tbsp. unsalted butter, melted
  Flaked sea salt
  Honey and butter

**1.** Preheat oven to 450°F. In a large bowl whisk together flour, maple sugar, baking powder, and kosher salt. Scatter cubed butter over. Using a pastry blender or your fingers, cut in butter until mixture resembles coarse crumbs with some pea-size pieces.
**2.** In a small bowl whisk together pumpkin and buttermilk. Stir into dry ingredients just until a soft dough forms. Turn onto a floured work surface; pat into a 1-inch-thick round. Using a 2-inch round cutter, stamp out biscuits. Repeat with scraps. Arrange on an ungreased baking sheet. Brush with melted butter; sprinkle with sea salt.
**3.** Bake 12 to 15 minutes or until golden brown. Serve warm or at room temperature with honey and butter. Makes 12 to 14 biscuits.
**EACH BISCUIT** *177 cal, 9 g fat, 24 mg chol, 494 mg sodium, 22 g carb, 3 g fiber, 4 g pro.*

**KRISTIN'S SCOOP**

What makes a welcome potluck dish? Meet these guidelines for a winner.

**IT WILL HOLD UP ON THE BUFFET**
"Consider dishes that are as delicious at room temperature as they are warm or chilled. Stick to sturdy salads rather than those with delicate greens that wilt quickly."

**IT HAS THREE COMPONENTS, MAX**
"Keep it simple. Dishes with multiple fillings, sauces, and garnishes are better saved for another time."

**IT'S CROWD-PLEASING WITH A HINT OF EDGE** "Your dish doesn't need to be bland, but this probably isn't the time for that new rabbit ravioli recipe you've been wanting to try. Think about putting a fresh twist on a dish you already know is a crowd-pleaser."

**WHAT CAN I BRING?** Give guests some guidance so you don't end up with 15 pumpkin pies. (Unless it's a pumpkin pie-theme potluck, of course.) Set up an online spreadsheet on Google Drive with categories (e.g., appetizers, vegetables, potatoes and casseroles, dessert, etc.); invite them to fill it in.

# PUMPKIN BUTTER-OATMEAL PIE

*Pumpkin butter is a matchmaker: it unites canned pumpkin and oats magically.*

**HANDS-ON TIME** 40 min.
**TOTAL TIME** 1 hr. 37 min

1   recipe Pastry for Double-Crust Pie (recipe, page 257)
1   egg, slightly beaten
1   Tbsp. water
½   cup butter
⅔   cup regular rolled oats
½   cup light-color corn syrup
3   eggs
1   9-oz. jar pumpkin butter
¾   cup canned pumpkin
1   tsp. vanilla
½   tsp. ground cinnamon
¼   tsp. ground nutmeg
⅛   tsp. salt
1   recipe Sweetened Whipped Cream (recipe, page 257) (optional)

**1.** Preheat oven to 450°F. Prepare pastry. On a lightly floured surface, roll half the pastry into a 12-inch circle. Line a 9-inch pie plate with pastry. Trim pastry even with edge of pie plate.
**2.** Roll remaining pastry half to ⅛ inch thickness. Cut into ¾- to 1-inch shapes with cookie cutters. For egg wash, stir together the beaten egg and the water. Brush edge of pastry shell with egg wash; arrange cutouts around edge. Brush cutouts with egg wash. Do not prick pastry. Line pastry with a double thickness of foil. Bake 8 minutes. Remove foil. Bake 4 to 5 minutes more or until crust is set and dry. Remove from oven. Reduce oven temperature to 350°F.
**3.** Meanwhile, for filling, in a large skillet melt 1 Tbsp. of the butter over low heat. Cook about 3 minutes or until golden brown; add oats. Cook and stir 3 to 4 minutes or until toasted; let cool.
**4.** In a large microwave-safe bowl microwave remaining butter 30 to 45 seconds or until melted. Stir in corn syrup; whisk in 3 eggs, the pumpkin butter, pumpkin, vanilla, cinnamon, nutmeg, and salt. Stir in oats. Pour filling into crust.
**5.** Cover edge of pie with foil to prevent overbrowning. Bake 45 to 50 minutes or until filling is set. Cool on a wire rack. If desired, serve with Sweetened Whipped Cream. Makes 8 slices.
**EACH SLICE** *594 cal, 33 g fat, 116 mg chol, 551 mg sodium, 68 g carb, 3 g fiber, 8 g pro.*

# HOME AGAIN

TV chef and cookbook author Vivian Howard cooks up her traditions at a Thanksgiving meal on the farm.

Since chef Vivian Howard was lured home to Kinston, NC, about 12 years ago, she has found her culinary voice, opened local restaurant Chef & the Farmer with husband Ben Knight, become host of the PBS character-driven documentary, "A Chef's Life," and has had her first cookbook published.

Vivian, who forged her career in big-name New York restaurants, brings modern sensibilities to Southern classic cooking for the couple's restaurants as well as for holiday celebrations. Her winning formula: Start with the familiar and introduce the unexpected. One example is her recipe for samosa appetizers—a technique she learned in New York that has been given a local twist with rutabaga and black-eyed peas. Most of the remaining Thanksgiving menu gets similar treatment. She cooks sweet potatoes with orange zest and brown sugar, then blends them smooth as apple butter to serve as a condiment with turkey. Cranberry relish has leeks and toasted pecans. And rather than traditional gravy, Vivian makes Warm Sorghum Vinaigrette, which she describes as a foolproof sauce for turkey.

"The only guarantees are turkey and stuffing," she says. "Everything else is up for grabs." Actually, even the stuffing has been reinvented as a rich gratin with turnips and greens along with crusty bread cubes and lots of cheese. For pumpkin dessert, Vivian serves cheesecake with a chai-spiced streusel. "I'm not a baker. And I figured out if I put streusel on just about anything it makes it good," she says.

Vivian further accommodates family tradition by setting out a cheese plate for her father, who wants something to eat upon arrival, and by entertaining

their 6-year-old twins, Flo and Theo, with the Thanksgiving Day Parade.

"Living and working here as an adult has proven to be such a huge gift," Vivian says. "I do think it's a

situation where I had to leave and live somewhere else to fully understand that this is where I belong. I'm grateful I figured it out."

## CRAB-FENNEL DIP

**HANDS-ON TIME** 30 min.
**TOTAL TIME** 1 hr. 30 min.

1    cup olive oil
1    fennel bulb, trimmed, quartered,
     cored, and cut into thin wedges
3    sprigs fresh tarragon
2    cloves garlic, smashed and peeled
2    tsp. crushed red pepper (optional)
3    cups grape tomatoes, halved if
     desired
1    cup mayonnaise
½    8-oz. pkg. cream cheese, softened
2    lemons, zested and juiced
1    tsp. ground fennel seeds
2    lb. lump crab, picked over for shells
1    cup grated Parmigiano-Reggiano
     cheese

**1.** Position a rack in the middle of oven;
preheat oven to 375°F. Butter a 2- to
2½-quart baking dish.
**2.** In a large saucepan combine olive oil,
fennel, tarragon, garlic, and, if desired,
crushed red pepper. Cook over medium
heat (oil should bubble gently) 10 minutes
or until fennel begins to soften. Add
tomatoes; cook 10 minutes more. (Fennel
should be soft but not mushy.) Remove
from heat; set aside.
**3.** In an extra-large bowl whisk together
mayonnaise, cream cheese, lemon zest
and juice, and ground fennel. Gently stir
in crab, cheese, and ½ tsp. salt. Using a
slotted spoon, transfer half the fennel-
tomato mixture to the crab mixture;
fold in gently, then spoon into prepared
baking dish or a 12-inch oven-going
skillet; set aside. Using a slotted spoon,
top with remaining fennel-tomato
mixture, reserving oil. Drizzle ¼ to ½ cup
of reserved oil over top. Bake 30 minutes
or until heated through and top is lightly
browned; cool slightly. Serve warm with
crackers. Makes 7 cups.
**PER ¼ CUP** *163 cal, 13 g fat, 45 mg chol,*
*287 mg sodium, 2 g carb, 1 g fiber, 9 g pro.*

## BLACK-EYED PEA SAMOSAS

**HANDS-ON TIME** 1 hr. 20 min.
**TOTAL TIME** 1 hr. 40 min.

1    lb. rutabaga, peeled and diced into
     ½-inch pieces (4 cups)
1    cup cooked or canned black-eyed
     peas, drained
½    cup onion, finely chopped
1    Tbsp. minced fresh ginger
3    cloves garlic, minced
2    Tbsp. vegetable oil
2    Tbsp. coriander seeds, toasted
     and ground*
1    Tbsp. cumin seeds, toasted and
     ground*
½    tsp. ground turmeric
¼    tsp. cayenne pepper
1    large tomato, diced, plus its juices
1    egg, beaten
1    11-oz. pkg. spring roll shells (such as
     Wei-Chuan brand)
⅓    cup butter, melted
     Cilantro-Buttermilk Dressing

**1.** For filling, in a 4-quart saucepan or
Dutch oven bring 2½ quarts water and
1 Tbsp. salt to boiling. Add rutabaga;
cook 30 to 35 minutes or until tender. Add
black-eyed peas during last 5 minutes.
Drain; set aside.
**2.** In a 12-inch skillet cook onion, ginger,
garlic, and ½ tsp. salt in oil 10 minutes
over medium heat, stirring occasionally
(do not let brown). Add all spices; cook
1 minute more. Stir in tomato and its
juices, cooked rutabaga and peas,
½ cup water, and 1 tsp. salt. Cook 5 minutes
or until mixture thickens and rutabaga
and peas have broken down a little;
cool completely.
**3.** For egg wash, mix together beaten egg
and 1 Tbsp. water; set aside. Slice shells in
half lengthwise to form two rectangles.
Using egg wash, join short ends of two
rectangles to create one long rectangle,
overlapping ends by at least ½ inch. Place
the rectangle on counter with short end
facing you.

**4.** Spoon about 2 Tbsp. filling onto one
corner of the nearest end. To form first
triangle, fold filled corner over so short
end aligns with opposite long edge.
(No need to turn filling upside down; it
should stay in place.) Continue folding
triangles the length of the rectangle like
you would a flag. Brush egg wash on end
of rectangle before the last fold, then
press onto triangle to seal. Place seam
side down on a baking sheet; repeat with
remaining wrappers and filling. Keep
samosas covered with a damp towel to
prevent drying out.
**5.** Preheat oven to 425°F. Brush both
sides of each samosa with melted butter,
then place 2 inches apart in two shallow
baking pans. Bake 15 minutes or until
golden, turning once. Serve with Cilantro-
Buttermilk Dressing. To make ahead, see
below. Makes 25 samosas.
**Cilantro-Buttermilk Dressing** In a
blender process ½ cup buttermilk, ½ cup
packed whole cilantro (stems and leaves),
2 Tbsp. mint leaves, 1 Tbsp. lemon juice,
and ¼ tsp. salt until smooth. Transfer to a
bowl. Whisk in ¼ cup plain Greek yogurt to
thicken. Makes about 1 cup.
**\*Tip** In a skillet toast seeds on low heat
2 minutes or until fragrant. Grind using a
mortar and pestle or spice grinder.
**Make-ahead** Chill baked samosas up
to 24 hours or freeze up to 1 month. To
reheat, preheat oven to 425°F. Place in a
shallow baking pan. Bake 10 minutes or
until filling is heated through.
**PER SAMOSA** *76 cal, 4 g fat, 14 mg chol,*
*227 mg sodium, 9 g carb, 1 g fiber, 2 g pro.*

CRAB-FENNEL
DIP

BLACK-EYED PEA
SAMOSAS

ROASTED
BRUSSELS
SPROUTS AND
GRAPES

TURNIP ROOT
AND GREENS
GRATIN

VIVIAN'S TURNIP GRATIN STANDS IN FOR TRADITIONAL STUFFING. FOR THE BRUSSELS SPROUTS DISH, SHE ROASTS RED GRAPES IN ONE PAN, THE SPROUTS AND SMOKED SAUSAGE IN ANOTHER.

## ROASTED BRUSSELS SPROUTS AND GRAPES

**HANDS-ON TIME** 10 min.
**TOTAL TIME** 25 min.

4   cups seedless red grapes
1   lb. Brussels sprouts, trimmed and halved (about 4 cups)
8   oz. link smoked sausage, sliced ½ inch thick
2   Tbsp. extra-virgin olive oil
3   Tbsp. Dijon-style mustard
2   Tbsp. lemon juice

**1.** Preheat oven to 425°F. Place grapes in a 15×10×1-inch baking pan. Place Brussels sprouts and sausage slices in a separate shallow pan. Drizzle each with half the oil; season each with ¼ tsp. each salt and black pepper. Toss to coat. Place pans on separate oven racks. Roast 15 to 20 minutes or until grapes are softened and juicy and Brussels sprouts are browned and tender, stirring once.
**2.** Meanwhile, for dressing, in a small bowl whisk together mustard and lemon juice. Transfer grapes and Brussels sprouts mixtures to a serving bowl, adding desired amount of pan juices and scraping up any browned bits from pan. Serve with dressing. Makes 8 servings.
**EACH SERVING** *194 cal, 12 g fat, 18 mg chol, 415 mg sodium, 20 g carb, 3 g fiber, 6 g pro.*

## TURNIP ROOT AND GREENS GRATIN

**HANDS-ON TIME** 1 hr.
**TOTAL TIME** 2 hr. 10 min.

2   Tbsp. plus 2 tsp. butter
3   medium onions, halved and sliced
3   turnips, peeled and cut into ½-inch cubes (3½ cups)
2   cups heavy cream
5   cloves garlic, thinly sliced
½   tsp. dried thyme, crushed
8   oz. turnip greens (4 cups)
1   egg
1   cup grated Parmigiano-Reggiano or Parmesan cheese
1   cup shredded Fontina or Gouda cheese
3   cups ½- to 1-inch dry bread cubes*

**1.** Preheat oven to 375°F. Coat the inside of a 2-quart oval or rectangular baking dish with 2 tsp. butter; set aside.
**2.** In a 10-inch skillet melt 1 Tbsp. butter. Add onions and ½ tsp. salt. Cook over medium heat, stirring frequently, until onions are caramelized and chestnut brown, about 30 minutes. (If the onions stick and pan bottom looks dark, add ⅓ cup water. Scrape up all the dark bits and cook until water is gone.) Transfer onions to a bowl; set aside. You should have ⅔ cup.
**3.** In a 6-quart pot bring heavily salted water to boiling. Add turnips; cook 2 to 3 minutes. Transfer turnips to a large bowl of ice water to stop the cooking. Once cool, drain and pat dry.
**4.** Meanwhile, in a 2-quart saucepan combine cream, garlic, and thyme; bring to just below simmering. Reduce heat to low; cook 30 minutes (do not let boil). Set aside; cool slightly.
**5.** In skillet used in Step 2 melt remaining 1 Tbsp. butter. Add turnip greens; cook 2 minutes or until greens wilt. Transfer to a colander; press out liquid. Transfer to cutting board; chop. Set aside.
**6.** In a large bowl whisk together cream mixture, onions, egg, cheeses, ½ tsp. salt, and ¼ tsp. black pepper. Stir in turnips, greens, and bread cubes. Transfer mixture to prepared baking dish. Let stand 10 minutes. (Or cover and chill overnight.) Bake, uncovered, 35 to 40 minutes or until center is bubbly and top is golden brown. Let stand 20 minutes before serving. Makes 8 to 10 servings.
**\*Tip** To make dry bread cubes, spread bread cubes in a 15×10×1-inch baking pan. Bake in a 300°F oven 10 to 15 minutes or until dry, stirring twice; cool. (Cubes will continue to dry and crisp as they cool.) Or let bread cubes stand loosely covered at room temperature 8 to 12 hours.
**EACH SERVING** *435 cal, 34 g fat, 129 mg chol, 803 mg sodium, 21 g carb, 3 g fiber, 12 g pro.*

"MY COOKING—AND MY THANKSGIVING—IS ROOTED IN MY NORTH CAROLINA LARDER BUT IS NOVEL ENOUGH THAT IT CALLS OUT TO THE REST OF THE WORLD." — VIVIAN HOWARD

BUTTER-ROASTED TURKEY,
SWEET POTATO BUTTER,
PECAN-CRANBERRY
RELISH, AND WARM
SORGHUM VINAIGRETTE
*Recipes on page 268*

# VIVIAN BALANCES THE MEAL'S RICHNESS WITH A SALAD OF CHARRED BITTER CHICORY AND SWEET PERSIMMONS.

## BUTTER-ROASTED TURKEY

*Photo on page 266.*

*The 2 pounds of butter—yes, really!— adds flavor, moistens the turkey, and ensures even browning.*

**HANDS-ON TIME** 30 min.
**TOTAL TIME** 3 hr. 50 min.

1   10- to 12-lb. turkey
1   orange, halved
4   sprigs fresh rosemary
4   sprigs fresh thyme
2   lb. unsalted butter
1   lemon, halved
1   2-foot square of 100-percent-cotton cheesecloth
1   recipe Pecan-Cranberry Relish
1   recipe Warm Sorghum Vinaigrette Persimmons

**1.** Preheat oven to 325°F. Remove giblets from turkey; rinse inside and outside well. Pat dry; season skin and cavity thoroughly with salt and black pepper.
**2.** Stuff cavity with orange, rosemary, and thyme. Twist wings under back; tie drumsticks together with 100-percent-cotton kitchen string. Place turkey in a roasting pan; roast 30 minutes. Meanwhile, place butter and lemon halves in a medium saucepan; melt over low heat. Transfer roasting pan to stove top. Fold cheesecloth in four layers. Using tongs, soak cheesecloth in butter. Drape cheesecloth over the breast. Repeat dipping and draping every 30 minutes; remove cloth for the final 30 minutes.* Roast 3 to 3½ hours or until a meat thermometer inserted in thigh registers 175°F. Let rest 20 minutes. Serve with Pecan-Cranberry Relish and Warm Sorghum Vinaigrette. If desired, garnish with whole persimmons and additional rosemary sprigs. Makes 8 to 10 servings.
**Pecan-Cranberry Relish** In a 10-inch skillet melt 2 Tbsp. butter. Add 1 cup chopped pecans; cook 3 to 4 minutes, stirring often to prevent burning. Add

⅔ cup dried cranberries, ⅔ cup sliced leeks, ¼ tsp. salt, and ⅛ tsp. black pepper. Cook and stir 2 minutes. Cover; keep warm. Makes about 2 cups.
**Warm Sorghum Vinaigrette** In a small saucepan melt 2 Tbsp. butter. Add a quarter of a red onion, minced, and ¼ tsp. salt. Cook until onion is soft. Add ½ cup cider vinegar, ¼ tsp. ground nutmeg, and ⅛ tsp. black pepper. Bring to boiling; add ⅓ cup sorghum syrup** and ¼ cup honey. Cook, uncovered, 25 minutes or until reduced by half. Serve immediately. (May be chilled up to 1 week. Reheat to serve.) Makes ⅔ cup.
**\*Tip** Or leave the cloth on breast throughout baking and baste or ladle lemon butter over.
**\*\*Tip** If unable to find sorghum, substitute equal parts molasses and honey.
**EACH SERVING** *612 cal, 31 g fat, 189 mg chol, 888 mg sodium, 32 g carb, 2 g fiber, 51 g pro.*

## SWEET POTATO BUTTER

*Photo on page 267.*

**HANDS-ON TIME** 15 min.
**TOTAL TIME** 1 hr.

2   lb. sweet potatoes
2   oranges (1 Tbsp. zest, ½ cup juice)
½   Tbsp. lime zest
½   Tbsp. lemon zest
⅓   cup butter, melted
3   Tbsp. packed light brown sugar
    Bottled hot pepper sauce

**1.** Preheat oven to 400°F. Scrub and prick potatoes; place in a pan lined with foil. Bake 45 minutes or until soft; cool 15 minutes. Cut in half lengthwise; scoop out pulp and discard skins.
**2.** In a food processor combine pulp, zests, orange juice, butter, sugar, 4 dashes hot sauce, and ½ tsp. salt. Process until smooth. Serve immediately with Butter-Roasted Turkey (see recipe, left). Or cover and chill up to 24 hours. To reheat and

serve, place in a large saucepan and heat over medium-low heat about 5 minutes, stirring often. Makes 8 servings.
**EACH SERVING** *166 cal, 8 g fat, 20 mg chol, 254 mg sodium, 23 g carb, 3 g fiber, 1 g pro.*

## PERSIMMON AND CHICORY SALAD

**TOTAL TIME** 45 min.

4   Fuyu persimmons, cut into 1-inch pieces
½   cup orange juice
¼   cup lemon juice
2   Tbsp. honey
½   tsp. crushed red pepper
2   Tbsp. unsalted butter
1   cup pecans, coarsely chopped
4   to 6 heads assorted chicories, such as Belgian endive, curly endive, and/or radicchio, quartered or cut into eighths
½   cup olive oil
½   cup shaved Pecorino Romano or Parmigiano-Reggiano cheese

**1.** In a medium bowl toss together persimmons, orange and lemon juice, honey, crushed red pepper, and ¼ tsp. salt; set aside.
**2.** In a large skillet heat butter over medium heat. Add pecans; cook and stir 3 to 4 minutes or until toasted. Remove from heat; season with ½ tsp. salt. Set aside.
**3.** Preheat a grill pan or cast-iron skillet over medium-high heat. Drizzle chicories with ¼ cup olive oil. Cook cut sides down 1 to 2 minutes or until charred. Transfer to a baking sheet or rack; let cool.
**4.** Drizzle remaining olive oil over persimmon mixture. To serve, arrange chicories in a single layer on a large platter. Top with persimmon mixture, toasted pecans, and shaved cheese. Makes 8 servings.
**EACH SERVING** *344 cal, 27 g fat, 13 mg chol, 324 mg sodium, 26 g carb, 5 g fiber, 4 g pro.*

PERSIMMON AND
CHICORY SALAD

# EVEN CHOCOLATE LAYER CAKE GETS A TWIST: IT'S FLAVORED WITH ORANGE ZEST AND BEETS, WHICH ADD MOISTNESS AND AN EARTHY COMPLEMENT.

## CHOCOLATE-ORANGE CAKE

*This cake has an unexpected ingredient: beets. Their earthy sweetness complements the richness of the chocolate.*

**HANDS-ON TIME** 40 min.
**TOTAL TIME** 1 hr. 30 min.

### CHOCOLATE-BEET CAKE

| | |
|---|---|
| 12 | to 16 oz. beets (about 3 medium) |
| | Nonstick cooking spray |
| 4 | oz. semisweet chocolate |
| 1 | cup vegetable oil |
| 1 | Tbsp. orange zest |
| 1 | Tbsp. vanilla |
| 1 | cup all-purpose flour |
| 1 | cup cake flour |
| 2 | tsp. baking powder |
| ¼ | tsp. salt |
| 3 | eggs |
| 1½ | cups granulated sugar |

### ORANGE SYRUP

| | |
|---|---|
| ⅓ | cup orange juice |
| ¼ | cup water |
| ¼ | cup granulated sugar |
| 2 | tsp. unsweetened cocoa powder |

### CHOCOLATE-CREAM CHEESE ICING

| | |
|---|---|
| 2 | 8-oz. pkg. cream cheese, softened |
| 12 | Tbsp. butter, softened (1½ sticks) |
| ⅓ | cup sour cream |
| ¼ | cup unsweetened cocoa powder |
| 2 | tsp. vanilla |
| 3 | cups powdered sugar |
| 2 | cups walnuts, coarsely chopped (optional) |
| | Kumquats (optional) |

**1.** In a 4-quart saucepan cover beets with water by 1 inch. Cover; bring to boiling over high heat. Cook at a rolling boil 30 minutes. Test beets for doneness by sticking a knife in the center of the largest one; knife should slide in with little resistance. Drain; cool completely. Peel and cube. Measure 2 cups.

**2.** Position a rack in the middle of the oven; preheat oven to 375°F. Coat three 8-inch round nonstick cake pans thoroughly with cooking spray.

**3.** In a small saucepan melt chocolate with ½ cup oil over low heat. In a blender blend the beets, remaining ½ cup oil, the orange zest, and vanilla until smooth; add melted chocolate. Pulse to combine; set aside.

**4.** In a medium bowl stir together the flours, baking powder, and salt; set aside.

**5.** In a large bowl beat eggs and sugar with an electric mixer on medium speed until light and fluffy, about 1 minute. Slowly add the chocolate-beet mixture until combined. Add dry ingredients in three batches, beating between each addition just until combined. (Batter will be thick.) Spoon a third of the batter into each prepared cake pan. Bake on the middle rack 15 minutes or until a toothpick inserted near the centers comes out clean. Remove cakes from pans; cool cakes upside down on racks 30 minutes.

**6.** For Orange Syrup, in a small saucepan whisk together orange juice, the water, sugar, and cocoa powder. Bring to boiling; cook, uncovered, until reduced by half. Once cake layers are cool, brush syrup over the bottoms of cake layers, using all the syrup.

**7.** For Chocolate-Cream Cheese Icing, in a bowl beat cream cheese, butter, sour cream, cocoa powder, and vanilla with an electric mixer on medium speed until velvety and soft. Beat in 3 cups powdered sugar, 1 cup at a time. (Vivian suggests lowering the speed at the start of each addition to avoid a mess.) Scrape bowl sides; if desired, stir in walnuts. Divide icing into thirds. Frost bottom layer, stack second layer, then third. If desired, top with kumquats. Makes 12 slices.

**PER SLICE** *931 cal, 61 g fat, 118 mg chol, 384 mg sodium, 93 g carb, 4 g fiber, 10 g pro.*

## OF ALL THE HOLIDAY COOKIES IN OUR ARCHIVES, THESE ARE MOST OFTEN GIVEN THE SPOTLIGHT.

### GINGER-SPICED COOKIES

**HANDS-ON TIME** 40 min.
**TOTAL TIME** 1 hr. 15 min.

½    cup shortening
⅓    cup sugar, plus more for rolling
1    cup mild-flavor molasses
2    Tbsp. milk
1    Tbsp. ground ginger
1    tsp. salt
1    tsp. baking soda
¼    tsp. ground cloves
¼    tsp. ground cinnamon
¼    tsp. ground nutmeg
2½    cups all-purpose flour
     Gold luster dust (optional)

**1.** Preheat oven to 350°F. Line two cookie sheets with parchment paper; set aside. In a large bowl beat shortening with a mixer on medium 30 seconds. Add ⅓ cup sugar; beat until light. Add molasses, milk, ginger, salt, baking soda, cloves, cinnamon, and nutmeg; beat until combined. Beat in flour until combined.
**2.** Shape dough into forty-eight 1¼-inch balls; roll in additional sugar to coat. Arrange 2 inches apart on prepared cookie sheets. Flatten slightly. Bake 10 to 12 minutes or until edges are firm. Remove; cool on a wire rack. If desired, brush on luster dust. Store in an airtight container at room temperature up to 3 days or freeze up to 3 months. Makes 48 cookies.
**PER COOKIE** *72 cal, 2 g fat, 78 mg sodium, 13 g carb, 1 g pro.*

### SPRITZ COOKIES

**HANDS-ON TIME** 30 min.
**TOTAL TIME** 1 hr.

1    cup butter, softened
1    cup granulated sugar
1    tsp. baking powder
½    cup plain Greek yogurt
1    egg
1    tsp. vanilla
½    tsp. almond extract
4    cups all-purpose flour
     Colored decorating sugar
     Edible silver dragées (optional)

**1.** Preheat oven to 400°F. In a large bowl beat butter with a mixer on medium for 30 seconds. Add sugar and baking powder; beat until light. Add yogurt, egg, vanilla, and almond extract; beat until combined. Gradually beat in flour until combined.
**2.** Using a cookie press fitted with desired disc, press dough 2 inches apart onto ungreased cookie sheets. Top with colored decorating sugar. Bake 7 minutes or until edges are light golden. Remove; if desired, top with edible silver dragées. Cool on wire racks. Repeat with remaining dough. Store in an airtight container at room temperature up to 3 days or freeze up to 3 months. Makes 130 cookies.
**PER COOKIE** *35 cal, 2 g fat, 5 mg chol, 22 mg sodium, 5 g carb, 1 g pro.*

### KRUMKAKE

*You can make cream filling up to 2 hours ahead; keep chilled. Shape cookies with the cone that comes with a krumkake iron. Fill only the cookies you plan to serve immediately; freeze unfilled cookies up to 3 months.*

**HANDS-ON TIME** 45 min.
**TOTAL TIME** 1 hr. 20 min.

1⅓    cups all-purpose flour
¼    tsp. salt
¼    tsp. ground cardamom
3    eggs
1    cup sugar, plus 3 Tbsp.
2    cups heavy cream
⅓    cup sour cream
1    tsp. vanilla
     Red food coloring (optional)
     Crushed peppermint candies (optional)

**1.** Grease and preheat krumkake iron press according to manufacturer's directions.
**2.** In a medium bowl whisk together flour, salt, and cardamom; set aside. In a large bowl beat eggs with an electric mixer on medium-high 3 minutes or until light in color. Gradually add 1 cup sugar, beating 2 to 3 minutes more or until thickened and lemon color. Alternately add flour mixture and 1 cup heavy cream to egg mixture, beating on low after each addition.
**3.** Spoon a rounded tablespoon of batter onto the iron press. Close; bake 60 seconds or until brown. Remove; quickly roll around cone. Let cool 5 seconds; remove. Cool completely on wire racks.
**4.** For cream filling to fill 12 Krumkake, in a large chilled bowl beat remaining 1 cup heavy cream, remaining 3 Tbsp. sugar, the sour cream, vanilla, and if desired, a few drops red food coloring on medium until stiff peaks form. Pipe or spoon into the 12 krumkakes just before serving. If desired, sprinkle with crushed peppermint candies. Double or triple cream filling recipe to fill additional krumkakes. Makes 36 krumkakes.
**PER KRUMKAKE** *159 cal, 11 g fat, 49 mg chol, 31 mg sodium, 13 g carb, 2 g pro.*

### SHORTBREAD STICKS

**HANDS-ON TIME** 20 min.
**TOTAL TIME** 1 hr.

1½    cups all-purpose flour
½    cup powdered sugar
⅔    cup butter
2    to 3 Tbsp. red decorating sugar

**1.** Preheat oven to 325°F. In a medium bowl stir together flour and powdered sugar. Using a pastry blender, cut in butter until mixture resembles fine crumbs and starts to cling. Gently knead into a ball (mixture may appear crumbly at first). On a lightly floured surface roll dough to a 12×5-inch rectangle. Sprinkle with red decorating sugar.
**2.** Cut dough crosswise into twelve 1-inch-wide strips. Arrange ½ inch apart on two ungreased cookie sheets. Bake 15 to 18 minutes or until edges begin to brown. Cool on sheets on wire racks 5 minutes. Transfer cookies to wire racks; let cool completely. Store in an airtight container at room temperature up to 1 week or freeze up to 3 months. Makes 12 cookies.
**PER COOKIE** *175 cal, 10 g fat, 27 mg chol, 82 mg sodium, 19 g carb, 2 g pro.*

## LEMON-CRANBERRY TASSIES

*Photo on page 290.*

**HANDS-ON TIME** 40 min.
**TOTAL TIME** 1 hr. 15 min.

½ cup shortening
1 cup packed brown sugar
1 Tbsp. vanilla
1 Tbsp. lemon zest
1 tsp. baking powder
½ tsp. baking soda
¼ tsp. salt
2 eggs
2½ cups all-purpose flour
¼ cup granulated sugar
1 cup purchased cranberry relish

**1.** Preheat oven to 350°F. In a large bowl beat shortening with an electric mixer on medium 30 seconds. Add brown sugar, vanilla, lemon zest, baking powder, baking soda, and salt; beat until combined. Beat in eggs until combined. Beat in flour until combined. Shape dough into 1-inch balls. Roll each ball in granulated sugar. Place each ball in a mini muffin cup; press into bottom and up the sides.
**2.** Bake 10 to 12 minutes or until golden. (If tassies puff during baking, press with spoon.) Cool 5 minutes in cups. Remove; cool on a wire rack. Repeat with remaining dough. Fill cooled tassies with cranberry relish. If desired, top with sugared cranberries and rosemary leaves. Makes 36 tassies.
**Make-Ahead** Store unfilled tassies in an airtight container at room temperature up to 3 days or freeze up to 3 months. Fill just before serving.
**PER TASSIE** *108 cal, 3 g fat, 10 mg chol, 56 mg sodium, 19 g carb, 1 g pro.*

## SUGAR COOKIE CUTOUTS

*Photo on page 290.*

**HANDS-ON TIME** 40 min.
**TOTAL TIME** 1 hr. 25 min.

1 cup butter, softened
1¼ cups sugar
1½ tsp. baking powder
½ tsp. salt
2 eggs
2 tsp. vanilla

3 cups all-purpose flour
1 recipe Royal Icing (*page 284*)
 Paste or liquid food coloring

**1.** In a large bowl beat butter on medium-high for 30 seconds. Add sugar, baking powder, and salt. Beat until combined, scraping sides of bowl occasionally. Beat in eggs, one at a time, and vanilla until combined. Beat in as much flour as possible; stir in remaining flour. Divide dough in half. Chill, covered, 30 minutes or until firm enough to handle.
**2.** Preheat oven to 375°F. On a floured surface, roll each dough half to ⅛- to ¼-inch thickness. Using cookie cutters, cut into shapes. Place 1 inch apart on ungreased cookie sheets.
**3.** Bake 7 minutes or until edges are firm and bottoms are light brown. Transfer to a wire rack; let cool.
**4.** To decorate, pipe Royal Icing around cookie edge. Flood inside the outline. Use a metal spatula to spread evenly; let dry completely. For painted designs, thin paste food coloring with water and apply using brushes or toothpicks. Store in an airtight container at room temperature up to 3 days or freeze up to 3 months. Makes 52 cookies.
**PER COOKIE** *80 cal, 4 g fat, 17 mg chol, 63 mg sodium, 10 g carb, 1 g pro.*

## APRICOT-BOURBON FRUITCAKE

*Fruitcake has always had a bit of a rep as a doorstop, deserved or not. BH&G has been tackling that bias for decades. This version— with dried (not candied) fruit—is sure to convert the naysayers.*

**HANDS-ON TIME** 1 hr.
**TOTAL TIME** 4 hr.

1 cup dry-roasted salted pistachios
2½ cups all-purpose flour
1 cup dried apricots, quartered
1 cup dried peaches, quartered
½ cup bourbon, plus more for drizzling
½ tsp. salt
½ tsp. baking powder
½ tsp. ground ginger
¼ tsp. baking soda
1 cup butter, softened
2 cups sugar

6 eggs
1 cup sour cream
¼ cup apricot nectar
2 tsp. vanilla
½ cup water
1 vanilla bean, split lengthwise
1 to 2 cups fruit, such as dried apricots, sliced kumquats, sliced oranges, and/or sliced grapefruit
 Fresh thyme sprigs

**1.** Preheat oven to 325°F. Grease and flour a 10-inch square tube pan or a 10-inch fluted tube pan; set aside.
**2.** In a food processor finely chop pistachios. Transfer to a small bowl; toss with ¼ cup of the flour. Add apricots and peaches to food processor; pulse until pea size. Transfer to a small bowl; add bourbon. Let soak 30 minutes, stirring to saturate fruit well.
**3.** In a large bowl combine remaining 2¼ cups flour, salt, baking powder, ground ginger, and baking soda; set aside.
**4.** In a large bowl beat butter 30 seconds with a mixer on medium-high. Gradually add 1½ cups of the sugar, beating 8 minutes or until fluffy. Add eggs, one at a time, beating 1 minute after each. With mixer on low, beat in sour cream, nectar, and vanilla. Add flour mixture, beating just until blended. Stir in nut mixture and soaked fruit with bourbon.
**5.** Pour batter into prepared pan. Bake 55 to 60 minutes or until a wooden toothpick inserted near center comes out clean. Cool in pan 10 minutes. Remove from pan. Cool completely.
**6.** Meanwhile, in a medium saucepan stir together remaining ½ cup sugar, the water, and vanilla bean. Bring to simmer over medium heat, stirring to dissolve sugar; cook 5 minutes or until syrup thickens slightly. Remove from heat; add fruit. Let stand 30 minutes.
**7.** Prick bottom of cake; drizzle with additional bourbon. Turn right side up. Spoon syrup over cake; top with fruit and thyme. Makes 16 slices.
**PER SLICE** *439 cal, 20 g fat, 107 mg chol, 266 mg sodium, 56 g carb, 3 g fiber, 7 g pro.*

APRICOT-BOURBON
FRUITCAKE

# SPICED COOKIE
# COTTAGE PATTERNS
*Photo on page 282.*

**ENLARGE ALL TO 200%**
**(11×17 PAPER)**

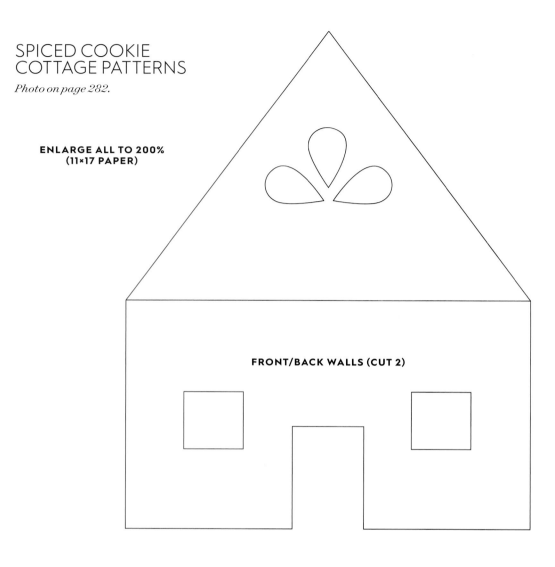

**FRONT/BACK WALLS (CUT 2)**

**FRONT PLANTERS (CUT 2)**

**SIDE PLANTERS (CUT 4)**

**ROOF (CUT 2)**

**AWNING (CUT 1)**

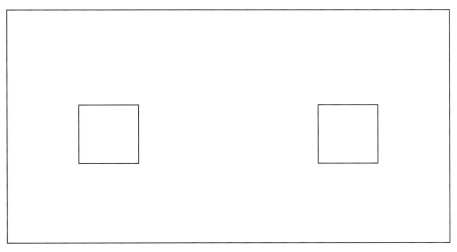

**SIDE WALL (CUT 2)**

# RECIPE INDEX

# METRIC INFORMATION

The charts on this page provide a guide for converting measurements from the U.S. customary system, which is used throughout this book, to the metric system.

## Product Differences

Most of the ingredients called for in the recipes in this book are available in most countries. However, some are known by different names. Here are some common U.S. American ingredients and their possible counterparts:

- Sugar (white) is granulated, fine granulated, or castor sugar.
- Powdered sugar is icing sugar.
- All-purpose flour is enriched, bleached, or unbleached white household flour. When self-rising flour is used in place of all-purpose flour in a recipe that calls for leavening, omit the leavening agent (baking soda or baking powder) and salt.
- Light-color corn syrup is golden syrup.
- Cornstarch is cornflour.
- Baking soda is bicarbonate of soda.
- Vanilla or vanilla extract is vanilla essence.
- Green, red, or yellow sweet peppers are capsicums or bell peppers.
- Golden raisins are sultanas.

## Volume and Weight

The United States traditionally uses cup measures for liquid and solid ingredients. The chart below shows the approximate imperial and metric equivalents. If you are accustomed to weighing solid ingredients, the following approximate equivalents will be helpful.

- 1 cup butter, castor sugar, or rice = 8 ounces = ½ pound = 230 grams
- 1 cup flour = 4 ounces = ¼ pound = 115 grams
- 1 cup icing sugar = 5 ounces = 150 grams

Canadian and U.S. volume for a cup measure is 8 fluid ounces (237 ml), but the standard metric equivalent is 250 ml.

1 British imperial cup is 10 fluid ounces.

In Australia, 1 tablespoon equals 20 ml, and there are 4 teaspoons in the Australian tablespoon.

Spoon measures are used for small amounts of ingredients. Although the size of the tablespoon varies slightly in different countries, for practical purposes and for recipes in this book, a straight substitution is all that's necessary. Measurements made using cups or spoons should always be level unless stated otherwise.

### Common Weight Range Replacements

| Imperial / U.S. | Metric |
| --- | --- |
| ½ ounce | 15 g |
| 1 ounce | 25 g or 30 g |
| 4 ounces (¼ pound) | 115 g or 125 g |
| 8 ounces (½ pound) | 225 g or 250 g |
| 16 ounces (1 pound) | 450 g or 500 g |
| 1¼ pounds | 625 g |
| 1½ pounds | 750 g |
| 2 pounds or 2¼ pounds | 1,000 g or 1 Kg |

### Oven Temperature Equivalents

| Fahrenheit Setting | Celsius Setting* | Gas Setting |
| --- | --- | --- |
| 300°F | 150°C | Gas Mark 2 (very low) |
| 325°F | 160°C | Gas Mark 3 (low) |
| 350°F | 180°C | Gas Mark 4 (moderate) |
| 375°F | 190°C | Gas Mark 5 (moderate) |
| 400°F | 200°C | Gas Mark 6 (hot) |
| 425°F | 220°C | Gas Mark 7 (hot) |
| 450°F | 230°C | Gas Mark 8 (very hot) |
| 475°F | 240°C | Gas Mark 9 (very hot) |
| 500°F | 260°C | Gas Mark 10 (extremely hot) |
| Broil | Broil | Grill |

*Electric and gas ovens may be calibrated using celsius. However, for an electric oven, increase celsius setting 10 to 20 degrees when cooking above 160°C. For convection or forced air ovens (gas or electric), lower the temperature setting 25°F/10°C when cooking at all heat levels.

### Baking Pan Sizes

| Imperial / U.S. | Metric |
| --- | --- |
| 9×1½-inch round cake pan | 22- or 23×4-cm (1.5 L) |
| 9×1½-inch pie plate | 22- or 23×4-cm (1 L) |
| 8×8×2-inch square cake pan | 20×5-cm (2 L) |
| 9×9×2-inch square cake pan | 22- or 23×4.5-cm (2.5 L) |
| 11×7×1½-inch baking pan | 28×17×4-cm (2 L) |
| 2-quart rectangular baking pan | 30×19×4.5-cm (3 L) |
| 13×9×2-inch baking pan | 34×22×4.5-cm (3.5 L) |
| 15×10×1-inch jelly roll pan | 40×25×2-cm |
| 9×5×3-inch loaf pan | 23×13×8-cm (2 L) |
| 2-quart casserole | 2 L |

### U.S. / Standard Metric Equivalents

| | |
| --- | --- |
| ⅛ teaspoon = 0.5 ml | |
| ¼ teaspoon = 1 ml | |
| ½ teaspoon = 2 ml | |
| 1 teaspoon = 5 ml | |
| 1 tablespoon = 15 ml | |
| 2 tablespoons = 25 ml | |
| ¼ cup = 2 fluid ounces = 50 ml | |
| ⅓ cup = 3 fluid ounces = 75 ml | |
| ½ cup = 4 fluid ounces = 125 ml | |
| ⅔ cup = 5 fluid ounces = 150 ml | |
| ¾ cup = 6 fluid ounces = 175 ml | |
| 1 cup = 8 fluid ounces = 250 ml | |
| 2 cups = 1 pint = 500 ml | |
| 1 quart = 1 litre | |